D1518704

RIGHTING CANADA'S
WRONGS

The Sixties Scoop
and the Stolen Lives of Indigenous Children

Andrew Bomberry and Teresa Edwards

JAMES LORIMER & COMPANY LTD., PUBLISHERS
TORONTO

James Lorimer & Company Ltd., Publishers
acknowledges funding support from the
Ontario Arts Council (OAC), an agency of the
Government of Ontario. We acknowledge the
support of the Canada Council for the Arts. This
project has been made possible in part by
the Government of Canada and with the support
of Ontario Creates.

Cover design: Gwen North

Library and Archives Canada Cataloguing in
Publication

Title: The Sixties Scoop and the stolen lives of
    Indigenous children / Andrew Bomberry and
    Teresa Edwards.
Names: Bomberry, Andrew, author. | Edwards,
    Teresa (Lawyer), author.
Series: Righting Canada's wrongs.
Description: Series statement: Righting Canada's
    wrongs | Includes bibliographical references
    and index.
Identifiers: Canadiana 20230237355 | ISBN
    9781459416697 (hardcover)
Subjects: LCSH: Sixties Scoop, Canada, 1951-ca.
    1980—Juvenile literature. | LCSH: Indigenous
    children—Canada—Juvenile literature. |
    LCSH: Indigenous children—Canada—Social
    conditions—Juvenile literature. | LCSH:
    Interracial adoption—Canada—Juvenile literature.
    | LCSH: Adopted children—Canada—Juvenile
    literature.
Classification: LCC HV875.7.C2 B66 2024 | DDC
    j362.734089/97071—dc23

Published by:
James Lorimer & Company Ltd., Publishers
117 Peter Street, Suite 304
Toronto, ON, Canada
M5V 0M3
www.lorimer.ca

Distributed by:
Formac Lorimer Books
5502 Atlantic Street
Halifax, NS, Canada
B3H 1G4
www.formaclorimerbooks.ca

Printed and bound in Korea.

Also in the Righting Canada's Wrongs series

Africville
An African Nova Scotian
Community Is Demolished
— and Fights Back

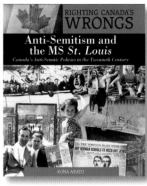

**Anti-Semitism and
the MS St. Louis**
Canada's Anti-Semitic
Policies in the Twentieth
Century

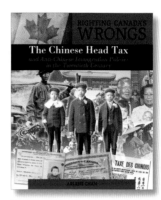

The Chinese Head Tax
and Anti-Chinese
Immigration Policies in the
Twentieth Century

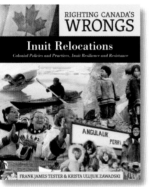

Inuit Relocations
Colonial Policies and
Practices, Inuit Resilience
and Resistance

**Italian Canadian
Internment**
in the Second World War

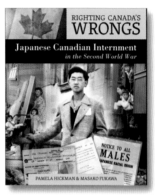

**Japanese Canadian
Internment**
in the Second World War

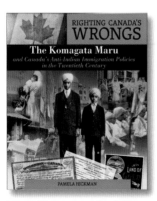

The Komagata Maru
and Canada's Anti-Indian
Immigration Policies in the
Twentieth Century

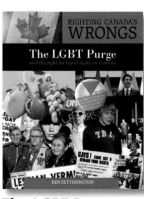

The LGBT Purge
and the Fight for Equal
Rights in Canada

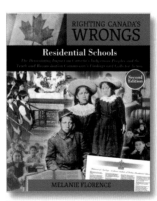

Residential Schools
The Devastating Impact
on Canada's Indigenous
Peoples and the Truth
and Reconciliation
Commission's Findings and
Calls to Action

Contents

Look for this symbol throughout the book for links to video and audio clips available online.

Visit www.lorimer.ca/wrongs to see the entire series

May this book foster peace and harmony among
all Nations for generations to come.
Miigwech, Niá:wen, Wela'lin, Meegwetch,
Nakumiik, Maarsii, Thank you, Merci.

— AB and TE

Foreword

My name is Adam North Peigan and I am the president of the Legacy of Hope Foundation (LHF) board of directors. I am a Survivor of the Sixties Scoop. The LHF is a national, Indigenous-led, charitable organization that has been working to promote healing and reconciliation in Canada for over twenty-two years. The LHF's goal is to educate and raise awareness about the history and impacts on seven generations of Indigenous (First Nations, Inuit and Métis) children, their families and communities from attending residential and/or day school and the subsequent Sixties Scoop. By developing understanding and addressing stereotypes, the LHF gives Canadians the tools to address discrimination and the ability to build respectful relationships, which contributes to the equity and dignity of Indigenous Peoples in Canada.

The LHF has exhibitions, curricula for K–12, workshops and podcasts for adults, along with activity guides and training, all aimed at educating Canadians about Indigenous history and the shared history of residential and day schools and the Sixties Scoop. The LHF works to develop empathy and understanding so as to eliminate racism against Indigenous Peoples and equip Canadians with the tools they need to become allies in fostering reconciliation in Canada.

I am pleased to provide this foreword to this book, which serves as an educational tool about a difficult chapter in the history of Indigenous Peoples in Canada. These events continue to have devastating impacts on Indigenous families. While we may all know about what happened to children at the hands of teachers, nuns, priests, coaches and those entrusted to care for them while at residential and day schools in Canada, this book addresses the injustices that occurred in the timeline of colonial oppression called the Sixties Scoop.

The Sixties Scoop occurred from 1951 to the early 1990s in Canada. Indigenous children from the First Nations, Inuit and Métis communities in Canada were forcibly removed by child welfare services and placed in non-native homes — primarily white homes — as permanent wards or for legal adoption as part of the extended forced assimilation against Indigenous Peoples.

The Sixties Scoop caused a lot of harm to generations of Indigenous Peoples. These children experienced multiple forms of violence and sexual abuse; physical, emotional and spiritual abuse; suffered from trauma and low self-worth; disconnection from family and all loving relationships, family norms, customs and traditions; and the loss of language, culture and overall loss of identity. Today we know that many children did not make it out alive from residential and day schools and the child welfare system. Their families, communities and Nations continue to grieve from those losses while others continue to heal from their experiences.

Since then, there has been a phenomenon known as the Millennium Scoop. In 2023 there were more Indigenous children in care with strangers than there were children in residential schools at its peak. There is more work to be done to address poverty among Indigenous Peoples, which is the primary reason children are removed from their families. Unfortunately, the current child welfare system will pay strangers to raise Indigenous children while the parents can't access financial support.

As a Survivor of the Sixties Scoop, I too suffered many losses as it was not a good time in my life. However, there is a lot of hope in Canada as the provincial governments of Manitoba, Alberta and Saskatchewan have made apologies to Survivors for the harm caused and the subsequent losses. The Government of Canada has begun providing financial compensation to Survivors for the harm caused by the Sixties Scoop. Today my personal story is about loss, strength, hope and overcoming.

Please take the time to read this book carefully as an opportunity to learn more about the Indigenous Peoples in Canada — there is more work to be done. I thank you for your time and your commitment to working toward reconciliation to address all of these injustices in Canada.

— Adam North Peigan, LHF Board President

CHAPTER 1

LIFE BEFORE THE SIXTIES SCOOP

Indigenous Diversity

Thousands of years before European settlers arrived, Indigenous Peoples lived throughout the land we now call Canada. There are three distinct Indigenous groups: Inuit, First Nations and Métis. Inuit traditionally lived in northern Canada, and First Nations lived mainly in the southern half of Canada. The Métis are descended from First Nations women and early European fishermen or fur traders. Each group had distinct languages, customs, ways of governing themselves and ways of educating their children. Indigenous societies formed extensive trade routes all across North America and had social, economic and political relationships with each other. They had complex systems in place and used traditional knowledge to live in harmony with the land, plants, trees, waterways, animals and birds. They have been and continue to be strong and resilient Peoples.

Watch the video at
https://tinyurl.com/The-Word-Indigenous

Inuit resourcefulness

Inuit adapted to their northern environment in many ways. They used animal bones to make tools, hides to make clothing and tents for summer and snow to make winter shelters, called igloos. This painting shows some Inuit with their dogsled. The dogs were raised and trained by each Inuit family. The handmade sleds moved easily across the ice. Dog teams pulled heavy loads during winter hunts and when Inuit moved camp between seasons.

Inuit snow house
In the winter, Inuit cut blocks of snow and built snow houses, like these ones, for shelter. When the weather turned warmer and the snow began to melt, Inuit adapted to their surroundings and moved into the traditional tents that they made.

Living with the land

There were over seventy-five different First Nations spread out in hundreds of communities across Canada. Each had adapted their lifestyle and practices to live comfortably in their territory. Before contact with Europeans, all First Nations had a deep understanding of the land, waters and animals in their area and they used these resources to help them survive throughout the year. This painting from 1838 shows a family of First Nations in what is now Quebec. They used natural materials like bark to make their canoe and animal hides to make their shelter.

Mi'kmaq resourcefulness on the East Coast

This painting shows a Mi'kmaw woman weaving a basket likely made from black ash, with the top made up of dyed porcupine quills for decoration. The Mi'kmaq lived on all types of seafood, freshwater fish, wild life such as moose and deer and local vegetation to sustain themselves. All of these materials were used to trade as well.

Animals were more than just food

This 1885 painting shows First Nations hunters working together to prepare several animals after a successful hunt. Gratitude and appreciation were a large part of hunting and preparing practices. It was common to make use of all of the animal. In addition to using the meat to feed many families, the hide would be used to make clothing and build their shelter. Many of the bones, antlers and hooves were used as tools, needles for sewing and other useful items to honour the lives that were taken and as a way of giving thanks for the animal's sacrifice.

European influence on traditional lives

Starting in the 1700s, many European fur traders travelled inland and traded with First Nations Peoples to access their furs. Contact and trade with non-Indigenous people began to influence some traditional ways of living for some communities. For example, this First Nations family is wearing European-influenced clothing.

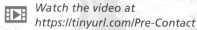

WATCH THE VIDEO

Watch the video at https://tinyurl.com/Pre-Contact

Métis families

Some Indigenous women married settlers and had families, eventually forming their own communities called the Métis. Métis have their own language, political structure, culture, songs and traditions. This Métis family was photographed at Fort Chipewyan, Alberta. Although Métis were found living across Canada in 2023, Alberta continued to have the highest Métis population. Their traditional territory is closely linked to the Red River in Manitoba and Saskatchewan.

Life before the Sixties Scoop

Wampum Belt

Some Woodlands First Nations used Wampum Belts, among other things, to demonstrate diplomatic agreements. Intricate beadwork on the belts represented important details about events, conflicts or people and agreements between nations. The belts are the European equivalent of a written treaty. They are examples of the sophisticated nature of Indigenous relationships and self-government that existed before European contact.

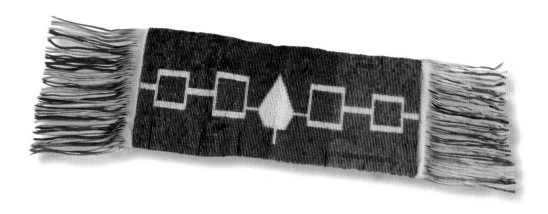

Distinct Métis style

Métis families often displayed a mix of First Nations and European styles, seen in this watercolour print from 1826. They are wearing soft leather moccasins common for many First Nations Peoples. The Métis drew upon their heritages to create a style unique to them. This emphasizes their creativity and agency. The man's vest and brightly patterned sash highlight intricate beadwork reflecting his pride in wearing traditional Métis clothing. The woman on the left is carrying a baby in a traditional cradleboard and smoking a long pipe, customs of her First Nations' heritage.

Family Life

Indigenous families were large, multi-generational groups who took care of each other, with everyone playing a valued role. Some changes came after generations of contact with settlers, including how they dressed, where they lived and how they lived, but many beliefs, teachings and traditions continue.

Multi-generational family
This photo from 1906 shows Mattagami First Nation women and children. Indigenous Peoples generally lived in multi-generational family structures where large families were able to share the work and responsibilities of day-to-day life. Many First Nations families continue this practice and have several generations living together and helping one another.

Fish stew
Inuit family groups worked hard to survive and thrive in the harsh northern climate. These Inuit are inside their family's igloo, warmly dressed in animal skins and furs. Big sister is making a pot of fish stew for the family and her little brother is ready to sample a bite. Older children were encouraged to look after and protect younger siblings or cousins. Siblings formed strong and loving bonds in childhood.

Daily life
On the left of this nineteenth-century painting, you can see a Mi'kmaw woman cooking lobster over a fire. The Mi'kmaq lived on seafood, freshwater fish, wildlife and local plants. This painting appears to be portraying trading with a settler.

Close family
The image below shows a Dene mother with a special hammock made with ropes and blankets. Wrapped up warmly and suspended off the cold ground, babies napped while their mothers worked nearby.

Older children were encouraged to look after and protect younger siblings and cousins. Siblings formed strong and loving bonds in childhood.

Lives changed after European contact

Canada's east coast is the traditional territory of the Mi'kmaq First Nation. They were among the first Indigenous Peoples to have contact with Europeans who came for fish and furs. By the time this family was photographed in 1890, the Mi'kmaq had lost much of their traditional territory due to colonization. This multi-generational family is dressed in European-style clothing. They are sitting in front of a traditional wigwam, a tent-like shelter that they covered in sheets of bark.

WATCH THE VIDEO

Watch the video at https://tinyurl.com/North-American-Networking

Over time, the effects of colonization on Indigenous families became more pronounced.

Colonization disrupted lifestyles

Over time, the effects of colonization on Indigenous families became more pronounced. By the 1940s when this photo was taken in Sturgeon Lake, Alberta, many First Nations were living in smaller family groups and in permanent homes. They no longer lived in large, multi-generational groups or travelled seasonally to hunt or fish. They had been forced onto remote reservations and had to give up their traditional lifestyles of hunting, fishing and gathering food from the land. This led many families into poverty and made it difficult for parents to provide a good life for their children.

Some adapted to European influences

This Cree family from Alberta was photographed in 1921. They are wearing European clothing but are still practising traditional Cree customs like growing their hair long and piercing their earlobes.

Education and the Role of Elders

WATCH THE VIDEO

Watch the video at
https://tinyurl.com/Education-Pre-Contact

Although Indigenous children may not have learned in a classroom, families passed on traditional teachings about the land, water, animals and winged ones throughout their lives. Children were taught by their families the skills they needed to survive on the land. They learned by watching others and by experience. Indigenous Peoples cultivated deep knowledge about the environment, with Elders and Knowledge Keepers playing key roles in their communities in order to live well and take care of each other.

As living connections to the ancient ways, language and culture of their people, Elders held important roles as teachers or knowledge keepers, healers, spiritual leaders or political advisors. They shared knowledge of animals and the land to ensure a successful hunt. Elders also provided spiritual guidance and conducted ceremonies. An Elder is not always a senior adult. They are a person in the community who is respected or who has special knowledge that is recognized by the community. They must be wise and committed to their cultural values and teachings. Elders must be good role models for community youth.

Traditional learning
As children grew older, they took on more responsibilities in their families and communities. More complex skills like basket weaving and chair making took years to learn. These Wolastoqiyik children in Perth, New Brunswick, are learning skills by watching the men.

Learning to sew
In this image, the young girl is learning how to make winter boots from an older relative.

Kids watched to gain experience
In this image, Inuit children in Qausuittuq, Nunavut (formerly called Resolute Bay), were learning to set a trap. Traditionally, Indigenous children learned by watching and through hands-on experience. There were no classrooms. Parents and Elders passed on knowledge, taught morals and values and taught children the skills they needed to survive on the land in harmony with nature.

Children were taught survival skills
Parents took children out on the land to teach them important survival skills such as hunting, trapping and fishing. Learning to clean, prepare and cook or preserve food were important skills children needed in order to support their own families one day.

Education and the Role of Elders

Trapping and hunting skills

Children learned how to get furs, prepare them and trade them for other important resources. The skills of trapping and hunting were considered culturally important long after the fur trade died out in the 1950s. These two men are pictured on Lac La Ronge, Saskatchewan.

Youth learned to help out

Rufus Goodstriker, a successful rancher on Kainai First Nation (Blood Reserve) in southern Alberta is shown here branding a horse with the help of his children. Traditionally, this kind of hands-on teaching allowed parents and Elders to pass on important skills and knowledge, while also increasing the number of helping hands in the community.

Parents took children out on the land to teach them important survival skills.

Cultural celebrations

Drum groups, like this one from the Northwest Territories in 1891, performed at feasts, special events and sports days. Some of these men were Elders, dressed in full regalia or ceremonial clothing. Each Indigenous group had their own styles of music and songs, passed from generation to generation, through the Elders of the community. Eventually the Government of Canada made it illegal for Indigenous Peoples to have spiritual and cultural practices. Many ceremonies continued but were done more secretly to not be caught by authorities.

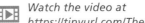
Watch the video at
https://tinyurl.com/The-Importance-of-Elders

Medicine man

Elders are the guardians of traditional knowledge, including knowledge about medicinal plants and how to heal many different illnesses. This medicine man lived in the Northwest Territories around 1900. As a healer, he dealt with physical ills like setting broken bones and treating fevers with medicinal plants and herbs. He also treated psychological ailments such as depression or anxiety. Common medicines used by some First Nations included sage, sweetgrass, cedar and tobacco, along with many other herbs and roots.

First Nations Elders

This image of Elders performing a ceremony in Kitwanga, British Columbia, in 1947 shows how Elders adapted to their changing world while continuing to practice and pass on important cultural practices. The three men in the background were wearing contemporary clothing, while singing and drumming traditional songs.

Education and the Role of Elders

Supporting Themselves

Traditionally, Indigenous communities supported themselves with the resources — plants and animals — around them. After contact with settlers, they began to trade furs and crafts, such as baskets, for items that made their lives easier, such as metal pots, fabrics and guns. The Government of Canada passed laws that limited the rights of First Nations to travel their traditional territories or to trade for economic purposes. Traditional practices, ceremonies, songs, dances and spiritual practices were made illegal. This greatly limited their ability to support themselves and forced many once-thriving nations into poverty. Some men were able to flee to work in the United States to help build bridges and construction projects to support their families. The government placed families on the roll to receive government assistance after taking away their economic independence, which led to malnutrition and poverty.

Inuit and trade

For many Inuit, the fur trade was an important part of their economy. This began in the mid-1800s and lasted until the 1950s. These Inuit women are standing outside a Hudson's Bay Trading Post in Igluligaarjuk (Chesterfield Inlet) in 1952. Inuit were skilled hunters and trappers. Many Inuit travelled long distances to these posts to trade furs for goods they could use in their daily lives. Some of these items would be traded again amongst Inuit who lived further away from the trading posts. The trading post was also an important place to meet up with other families.

A paying job

Some Indigenous women worked for wages at whatever jobs were available to support their families. Sometimes they were hired to be caregivers, but Canadian society still held racist attitudes and negative opinions about Indigenous parenting ways. Karjurjuk is seen here carrying a baby while doing household tasks and other work. She was hired to care for the baby of the Hudson's Bay Company agent near her home in Qamanittuaq, Nunavut (formerly known as Baker Lake). Her young charge seems quite happy to ride along on her back, kept warm by her body heat. Karjurjuk was probably responsible for feeding and comforting the baby, as well as any other household tasks her employer gave her during the day.

Local resources were destroyed

Traditional Indigenous economies were based on living sustainably, in sync with seasonal changes and animal migration patterns. Native plants and animals supported huge communities across Canada. As settlers converted land for agriculture, Indigenous Peoples were denied access to many precious resources. On the prairies, settlers deliberately slaughtered the plains bison, depriving local Indigenous Peoples of their most important economic resource. By the early 1900s, many of them were struggling to survive. This Cree family went to work on a sugar beet farm in Alberta to earn money to feed their family.

Indigenous agriculture

Oneida First Nations were part of the larger Iroquois Confederacy, also called the Haudenosaunee. They were excellent farmers and traditionally planted large crops of corn, beans and squash. They referred to these plants as the "Three Sisters" because they grew so well together. Knowledge of how to grow these plants was passed down from generation to generation. This image from 1912 shows a hard-working Oneida farmer and his wife after a long day in the field.

Harvesting wild rice

Gathering resources for food and trade involved both adults and children. This Anishinaabe man and youth are harvesting manoomin (wild rice) in Lac Seul, Ontario. Manoomin was an important food for many First Nations. Wild rice is not actually rice; it is the seed from a marsh grass. Two experienced harvesters could bring in 600–800 pounds of manoomin per day!

Processing wild rice

After the rice was harvested and allowed to dry for a few days, it was picked through to remove debris. It was then "parched" in metal cylinders over a fire to help loosen the shell, also known as the "hull" of the seed. The young girl on the right is learning many important skills while she helps her mother. Together they will parch, hull and eventually bag the rice to be stored for the family, shared within the community or traded for other goods.

Basket weaving

Many Indigenous women were highly skilled at making baskets of every size and shape. Basket makers were important members of the community since well-made baskets were needed for gathering and storing plants, transporting goods, and for laundry. Baskets also became an important trade item, thereby contributing to the Indigenous economy. Baskets were made from materials found in nature like grass, bark or even animal skins. This Anishinaabe woman is making a birchbark basket.

Setting a trap

As well as hunting larger animals, First Nations often used trap lines to capture smaller animals such as rabbits. This photo from 1908 shows an Indigenous man setting a muskrat trap. He used the furs mainly for trade.

Tobacco harvesting

Charlie King of Wiikwemikoong First Nation on Manitoulin Island, Ontario, proudly shows off his tobacco at harvest time. Traditionally, tobacco was an important medicine for most First Nations people, often used for ceremonies or for trade. By the 1940s it was also a valuable crop to grow and sell. Many First Nations farmers grew tobacco. Young Indigenous men worked on other large tobacco farms during the summer months to earn money.

Labour

Indigenous men began leaving their areas to find work in the construction of roads, bridges and skyscrapers in both Canada and the United States. These Indigenous men were part of a work crew that cleared land outside of Yellowknife, Northwest Territories, for a new road in the winter of 1960. More than 150 Indigenous men were hired for the project. Some of the men came from faraway communities to find work. Foreman Andre Martin, seen in the foreground, and others spent the winter working in the bush and sent their wages back to their families.

CHAPTER 2

INFRINGEMENT OF RIGHTS

Colonial Attitudes, Policies and Racism

Watch the video at https://tinyurl.com/Canada-and-Their-Promises

Settler colonialism is a type of colonialism where people come to settle in a land while, at the same time, displacing people who were already there. Canada is based on settler colonialism.

In 1876, the Government of Canada created the Indian Act. It was the beginning of a series of laws and policies that controlled Indigenous Peoples — where they lived, how they lived and how their children could be raised. Government agents known as Indian Agents enforced the laws of the Indian Act in most communities. Many of these laws were written to control First Nations and to remove them from their traditional territories and their resources. The Indian Act was amended many times. Government laws, policies and programs worked to achieve an overarching goal to control all lands and resources in Canada.

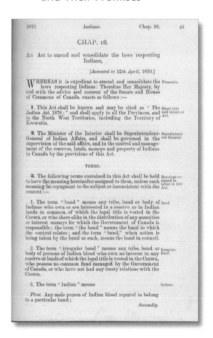

Indian Act
In 1876 the Canadian government passed a collection of laws called the Indian Act, which gave them sweeping control over First Nations identities, governance, religion, cultural practices and education. It restricted many First Nations to reserve land. Government Indian Agents enforced the laws of the Indian Act in most communities. Over the years, the Indian Act was updated and changed. It did not always include Inuit, and in 1951 they were specifically excluded.

Watch the video at https://tinyurl.com/What-Is-the-Indian-Act

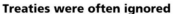

Treaties were often ignored
Treaties were agreements between First Nations and colonial governments. This treaty medal from the late 1800s represented commitments made between First Nations and the British Crown. Treaties dealt with the use of land and resources, as well as guidelines for living peacefully. Unfortunately, as time went on and more settlers arrived, treaty rights were often ignored in order to remove Indigenous Peoples from their land and limit their rights in society.

Free land for settlers

Through treaties, the government took over huge areas of fertile land in what is now Manitoba, Saskatchewan and Alberta. To attract settlers, the government advertised with colourful posters like this one. Men could get 160 acres of free land for farming or ranching. Immigration laws favoured British or northern European people. Indigenous populations declined from 1890 to 1930. Factors included introduced diseases and poverty.

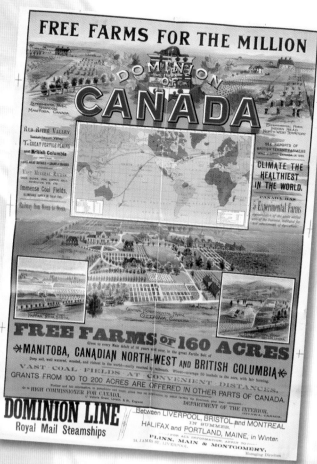

Sacred ceremonies banned

From 1884 to 1951, the Indian Act outlawed sacred ceremonies and practices such as the potlatch, sun dance, sweat lodge, etc. People were arrested for performing them and their ceremonial materials were taken away by the RCMP or Indian Agents. The effects of this prohibition are still felt today as generations were robbed of their traditions, practices, spirituality and connections to the land. For example, on the west coast, potlatches brought communities together to redistribute wealth in the form of gifts. They were also a time to strengthen relationships between families and communities. Despite the ban, some communities continued to hold potlatches in secret. In 1903, these Nisga'a leaders, dressed in full regalia, risked being arrested at this potlatch.

Converted to Christianity

Churches, like this one on the Peguis Reserve in Manitoba, were set up by missionaries to convert First Nations Peoples to Christianity. Many missionaries also taught religious lessons to the children in the community. Colonial society viewed Christianity as "civilized." The many sacred Indigenous spiritual practices were viewed as "savage."

Colonial Attitudes, Policies and Racism

Discrimination against First Nations women

Starting in 1869, the Indian Act discriminated against First Nations women. It stated that a woman's status depended on her husband. Women who married a man who wasn't First Nations lost their status, as did any children they had. They were no longer considered First Nations. They couldn't live on treaty land and were abandoned by the government. Non-Indigenous women who married First Nations men became "Indians" under the Indian Act until 1980, while Indigenous women were fighting to have their status reinstated.

(1.) Any Indian who may be admitted to the degree of Doctor of Medicine, or to any other degree by any University of Learning, or who may be admitted in any Province of the Dominion to practice law either as an Advocate or as a Barrister or Counsellor or Solicitor or Attorney or to be a Notary Public, or who may enter Holy Orders or who may be licensed by any denomination of Christians as a Minister of the Gospel, shall *ipso facto* become and be enfranchised under this Act.

Forced to enfranchise

This excerpt from the Indian Act explains that an Indigenous person who chose any of these professions lost their Indigenous identity, rights and claims. They became Canadian citizens instead. Sadly, even when enfranchised, they were often still discriminated against by society at large.

First Nation resistance

Despite the ban on Indigenous cultural practices, some groups continued to show resistance to colonial oppression. This picture of a Powwow was taken in 1930 in Treaty 6 territory (Alberta) during the ban. Sacred objects, ceremonial pipes or regalia like the headdresses worn here were often confiscated by authorities and sold to museums or destroyed.

Communities were relocated

Sometimes the government forced communities to relocate from their traditional territories to make way for white settlers or infrastructure, like dams or railroads. Often the new location was less desirable and there was less game to hunt for food. This Sayisi Dene family from Caribou Post, Manitoba, was forced to relocate closer to Churchill in 1935. They suffered terrible hardship. Within two years of relocating, half of the community had died, primarily of hunger and exposure.

Forced onto reserves

Like most First Nations, the White Cap First Nation were forced onto reserve lands in 1881. Chief Wapahaska (White Cap) and his people settled on the banks of the South Saskatchewan River and farmed or worked for wages in the nearby town of Prince Albert. By the 1920s when this photo was taken, many First Nations had been forcibly removed from their traditional hunting and harvesting grounds by the government, allowing for more settlers to take them over and for the construction of roadways and railways.

Reserves were not really protected

Even though reserve land was supposed to be protected, the Canadian government updated the Indian Act in 1918 to give itself the power to lease it out to non-Indigenous people. Families, like this one on Red Earth Reserve, Saskatchewan, in the 1930s, found their land base shrinking. This made it harder to provide for their families.

The pass system

In 1885 a pass system was implemented to control First Nations people from moving around on their own lands. A First Nations person could not leave their reserve unless they had permission, a pass, from the Indian Agent who was assigned to oversee the reserve. This pass, issued in 1932, gave a man named Edward, from Duck Lake, permission to leave the reserve to hunt and trap for food for two weeks.

RCMP began policing reserves

The RCMP are the federal police service. They were authorized to police the day-to-day activities of those on reserve and many RCMP still do today. Sam Crow (right), the Innu post manager for the Hudson's Bay Company outpost in Richmond Gulf, Quebec, is seen here with his family and RCMP Constable Van Blarcom.

Colonial Attitudes, Policies and Racism

Residential Schools

Many First Nations were pressured to send their children away to the church-run residential schools. This practice began in the early 1800s and continued until 1996.

In 1920, the Government of Canada made it law that all First Nations children ages seven to fifteen had to attend. However, children as young as three and as old as seventeen were taken away to the schools. The schools were run by the church administrators, nuns and priests, but were paid for by the Government of Canada. The goal was to remove all that was Indigenous from each child and to destroy all ties to family, language, culture, spirituality and traditional practices. Instead, children were to be taught English, French and religion and had to engage in manual labour for the churches.

Seven generations of Indigenous children were subjected to all forms of abuse — physical, sexual, mental, spiritual and emotional. Many still suffer with depression, flashbacks, night terrors, trauma disorders and addictions as a result.

Children were taken

This 2017 Kent Monkman painting, called *The Scream*, depicts the trauma First Nations parents and children experienced when children were forcefully taken away by RCMP and church authorities. The RCMP also searched for runaway students and returned them to school. Indigenous parents who did not bring their children to residential schools were fined. Some families chose to try and blend in to settler society and moved away in order to keep children out of residential schools. Anywhere they moved, as soon as they were identified as Indigenous, the children were taken to a residential school in that area.

WATCH THE VIDEO

Watch the video at
https://tinyurl.com/Stolen-Words

Control and destruction of First Nations

Duncan Campbell Scott became the federal Deputy Minister of Indian Affairs in 1913. He studied the industrial school system in the US designed to gain control over First Nations families there and brought the idea to Canada. He actively pursued policies that limited the rights of First Nations, Inuit and Métis and was the key person pushing forward the residential school system in Canada.

Forced by law

This is an excerpt from the 1920 amendment to the Indian Act, which made it mandatory for every First Nations child aged seven to fifteen to attend residential school.

Poor nutrition at school

The Mohawk Institute Residential School (left) opened in 1831 in Brantford, Ontario. It earned the name "The Mush Hole" because of the tasteless porridge that was often the only food fed to the children. Many schools did not provide enough nutritious food for the children.

Their hair was cut

When children first arrived at school they were stripped of their own clothing, bathed and treated for lice whether they had them or not. Their hair was cut short in the same style. Most First Nations have sacred teachings about hair, so cutting it off was extremely violating. The church staff cut off children's hair in an attempt to erase their personal identity. Notice how the children have identical haircuts and are wearing similar clothing.

Punished for speaking their own language

Most residential schools in Canada were run by the Catholic Church, but others, such as the Anglicans, were also involved. Personal items were taken from the children as soon as they arrived. Children were forbidden to speak their own language and severely punished and abused if they did. The idea was to abuse them until they finally only spoke English or French.

Children were assigned a number and were referred to by that number and not their traditional or birth name. They were also forbidden to speak to their own siblings.

Poor education

This class of Mi'kmaw girls was learning to sew. Sewing, kitchen duties and working in the school's laundry were common activities for girls. Boys worked in the gardens or fields and were forced to do other manual labour. Students were forced to spend more time working than they were allowed to spend in the classroom learning. More than 40 percent of the teachers had no formal training in education and were not qualified teachers.

Without a proper education, these young adults had few skills to sustain themselves, especially if they attempted to go to cities where they often faced discrimination. They often felt that they could not return to their community and family, because they had been disconnected from them for years and had been told regularly, if not daily, that "those people" were inferior and evil.

Money misused

Pictured here are students and staff of the Fort Providence Mission School in the Northwest Territories in 1929. It was one of the first residential schools to open in the North. Funding for the children was often used to pay for expenses within the church and was not allocated to the support and well-being of the children. In some instances, children went without fruit, milk, cheese, meat and eggs even though the schools had farms attached to them and were surrounded by apple orchards that the children were forced to work.

Schools overcrowded, children neglected

The churches received funding for each child that attended the school, and the dormitories were often overcrowded. Illnesses such as influenza, pneumonia and tuberculosis spread more quickly than usual through the student population due to malnutrition and poor living conditions.

Often sick children did not receive adequate care or medical treatment while suffering already from malnutrition, and they died needlessly at school. Other children died from abuses and accidents.

School administrators began burying students on the property of the schools. Some were in cemeteries and some had unmarked graves. Some parents were not informed that their child died until the end of the school year and were unable to provide a proper burial or ceremony.

Sports day at school

This photo shows an annual sports day at Battleford Residential School in Saskatchewan. Indigenous Peoples traditionally played games, had sports contests and engaged in dancing for fun and fitness. In an effort to further erase ties to their culture, students were not allowed to play traditional games like lacrosse. Games and sports that were seen as more "Canadian," like hockey, were played on sports days at school. Ironically, there is now evidence that hockey originated from a similar game called Alchamdyk, played by the Mi'kmaq for generations.

Hockey champs

By the 1950s, some schools allowed students to participate in extracurricular activities. Hockey was popular in Canada, and some schools formed teams that competed against other schools in the area. This team from Maliotenam, Quebec, proudly posed with their championship trophies.

Although playing hockey provided some refuge for students, many were subjected to discrimination by other teams when playing against them. Many students have since come forward to recount the abuses they experienced by priests and coaches during their time playing hockey.

Poorly qualified teachers

The remote locations of many residential schools, and the low wages they offered, made it difficult to attract well-trained, qualified teachers. Some teachers had almost no qualifications but instead were hired for their religious zeal. Despite being at school, many students received very little actual educational classroom time and the level of instruction was often poor.

Early mission schools in the North

Mission-run schools operated in northern communities for over a hundred years before the Government of Canada took over the education of Inuit in 1949. These children posed with their teacher, Father Trinell, outside the mission school in Kinngait (Cape Dorset), Northwest Territories.

Sir Joseph Bernier Federal Day School

This is the federal day school in Igluligaarjuk (Chesterfield Inlet), in what is now Nunavut. The school officials and the hostel staff, as Turquetil Hall, perpetrated some of the worst physical, psychological and sexual abuse on Inuit children who were students.

Dr. Peter Henderson Bryce

Dr. Peter Henderson Bryce was a public health official for the Government of Canada. He studied the health and well-being of children in residential schools from 1905 to 1906. He was appalled by the high rates of illness, malnutrition, injury and death for students. His reports were ignored by the government for years, but he eventually published his findings at his own expense in 1922.

Watch the video at
https://tinyurl.com/Peter-Bryce

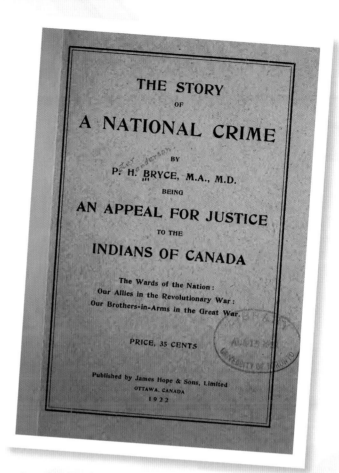

THE STORY
OF
A NATIONAL CRIME
BY
P. H. BRYCE, M.A., M.D.
BEING
AN APPEAL FOR JUSTICE
TO THE
INDIANS OF CANADA

The Wards of the Nation:
Our Allies in the Revolutionary War:
Our Brothers-in-Arms in the Great War.

PRICE, 35 CENTS

Published by James Hope & Sons, Limited
OTTAWA, CANADA
1922

"A National Crime"

Dr. Bryce's report (above) was titled *A National Crime*. He outlined his findings in the residential schools that he studied. He estimated that as many as one out of every four students attending a residential school would die. Although Dr. Bryce made the Government of Canada aware of the conditions and the multiple health risks and risks of death to children, there was little improvement in conditions. The schools remained open for another seventy-five years. More generations of Indigenous families experienced multiple forms of abuse, profound loss and estrangement from family life and relationships, language, culture, spirituality and traditions.

Unsafe housing conditions

This is a 1945 photo of St. Cyprian's Indian Residential School in Brocket, Alberta. Many schools were poorly insulated and were cold in the winter and hot in the summer. This one had fire escapes, but many didn't. Students were trapped if there was a fire.

Impacts of Residential Schools

WATCH THE VIDEO

Watch the video at
https://tinyurl.com/
Residential-School-Timeline

The impacts of residential schools on the Survivors and their families are complicated. Many students suffered abuse, loss of language and culture, distancing from families and lack of nurturing and nutrition. Many Survivors have spoken of difficulties with parenting, inability to pass down traditional ways, chronic malnutrition and physical abuse. The impacts are long term and have affected many generations.

Some parents resisted

Parents who had attended residential schools themselves knew of the abuse and poor conditions. They did not want to send their children away to suffer the same trauma. This newspaper article from 1927 describes a fight that broke out between parents and the RCMP. The parents were arrested and fined for refusing to send their children to school.

INDIANS ATTACK MOUNTED POLICE

Refused to Send Children to School—Warrants Issued For Arrest

PUT UP FIGHT

Men and Women Join in Melee—Several Injured —Lenient Sentences

Arising out of the refusal of several Indians on the reserve to send their children to school and an effort on the part of the officers of the Royal Canadian Mounted police to serve them with warrants for arrest, charges under section 169 of the Criminal Code of Canada of interfering with the police in the discharge of their duty were laid against Francois Timoyakin, George Lessard, Cosmus Sam, Julia Manuel and (Continued on Page Three)

Survivors suffered many negative impacts

Survivors of residential schools experienced or witnessed many acts of abuse, harsh punishments, neglect and even death. Repeated childhood trauma and abuse meant it was difficult for Survivors to develop healthy parenting skills. Rates of depression, mental illness and drug addiction were high among parents who attended these institutions. Many Survivors suffered post traumatic stress disorders, depression, flashbacks and night terrors.

WATCH THE VIDEO

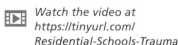
Watch the video at
https://tinyurl.com/
Residential-Schools-Trauma

Schools disrupted cultural identity

At school Indigenous children were taught religion, English or French and manual labour. The children were removed from familial relationships and bonds, community connections, their language, traditions and culture. This clashed with their traditional ways of being, cultural parenting practices and ways of relating to the world.

Disconnected from family life

Students were disconnected from the normal routines of family life, family relationships, love and comforts from home, and from the cultural connections in their community. As a result, many Survivors had difficulty adjusting to life outside of residential school and had difficulty communicating and having healthy relationships as adults.

Punished for their traditional beliefs

These students, from St. Paul's Hostel in Yukon, were headed to church. Since residential schools were run by churches, religious instruction was a major part of student life. Children attended mass every day. Indigenous spiritual teachings were viewed with hostility and shame, and anyone practising them was at risk of being criminalized. Traditional beliefs and practices were eventually outlawed.

Long-term health problems

It was common for residential schools to have a garden or field for growing fresh food. Unfortunately, the food was often sold to make money for the church. Children who worked in the fields rarely got to enjoy what they harvested. Malnutrition and illness were common, and students often did not receive proper medical treatment. Some schools had apple orchards or farms, but students were forbidden to eat the fruit, meat, milk, eggs, etc. that they farmed, even if there was food left rotting on the ground.

 Watch the video at https://tinyurl.com/Aboriginal-Healthcare

Families were kept apart

Children were taken away to schools as young as three years old. Brothers and sisters were not allowed to speak to each other at school because boys and girls were generally kept separate. Even same-sex siblings were kept apart to destroy all that was Indigenous and to dismantle cultural identity and family bonds. Many Survivors had difficulty parenting based on the abusive and dysfunctional experiences they lived through at the hands of nuns, priests, teachers, coaches and administrators.

Many Survivors couldn't bond with their children later in life or didn't know how to express feelings or affection. This led to more generations of children being impacted by the abuses their parents experienced. This began the era of inter-generational trauma.

Many Survivors couldn't bond with their children later in life.

Watch the video at https://tinyurl.com/Cycle-of-Trauma

Most parents could not visit
This image of Two Horns and his family was taken at the Regina Indian Residential School in Saskatchewan. The two small children in front belonged to school staff. Unfortunately, schools were often so far away that parents could not visit. Many children, their parents and families suffered great sadness being separated from one another for such long periods. Some children stayed for up to ten years without ever seeing their family, particularly if their school was several provinces away.

Schools were often so far away that parents could not visit.

Inuit families adapted their traditional lifestyle
In order to stay close to their children who were forced to attend federal day schools, many Inuit families followed their children to school in settlements. This Inuit family set up a camp near the school at Mittimatalik (Pond Inlet). Many were forced to give up some of their traditional practices of moving camps seasonally to follow game for trapping and hunting to be near their children.

CHAPTER 3

THE SIXTIES SCOOP (1951–1985)

Authority to Judge

As the Government of Canada slowly moved away from residential schools as a way to separate Indigenous children from their families, child welfare agencies and social workers became the new method for taking the children out of their homes. Social worker associations had lobbied the Canadian government to apply their skills to Indigenous communities. In 1951, the Indian Act was amended to give provincial child welfare agencies access to on-reserve Indigenous families. Not long after the amendment, welfare agencies began taking more and more children in what became known as the Sixties Scoop.

88. Subject to the terms of any treaty and any other Act of the Parliament of Canada, all laws of general application from time to time in force in any province are applicable to and in respect of Indians in the province, except to the extent that such laws are inconsistent with this Act or any order, rule, regulation or by-law made thereunder, and except to the extent that such laws make provision for any matter for which provision is made by or under this Act.

— 1951 Indian Act Amendment

This is an amendment to the Indian Act, the supreme law for Indigenous Peoples in Canada. Inuit were brought under the Act for the first time in 1951.

Residential schools slowly replaced
Sadly, thousands of children never returned home from residential school. They died of diseases they would not normally have died from. Due to malnutrition, they were more at risk of dying. They also died of abuse, neglect and murder. This 2018 painting is by Isaac Murdoch, an Ojibwe artist from Serpent River First Nation in Northern Ontario. It's called *The Ones Who Stayed.*

Provinces get involved
In 1951, the Liberal government under Prime Minister Louis St. Laurent, pictured here, decided to advance an aggressive assimilationist policy to make Indigenous Peoples just like Canadians. This meant increasing ways to put Indigenous Peoples under provincial laws.

Lack of health care

Before 1951, most Indigenous settlements or reserves did not have health care facilities. This meant that if Western medical care was desired, it needed to be specially arranged. It is important to remember that this did not mean that communities were without medicines; only that there was not ready access to Western doctors.

Some social workers did not respect traditional medicines or treatments and saw Indigenous communities as lacking in health care. When family and community situations did not resemble their expectations, child welfare agents were more likely to remove children from the home.

This is an image of a child being examined by Dr. T.J. Orford, who was the doctor and agent for the James Bay district.

Inadequate training

In 1947, many social workers viewed Indigenous Peoples as having a cultural deficit; their cultures and lifestyles were inferior to non-Indigenous people. This is in part because Indigenous families did not look or behave like a traditional Western family.

Most social workers, like the one pictured below, believed their interventions were helping, but they did not have adequate training. They were without knowledge or understanding of residential school trauma, or the struggles caused by lack of resources and loss of land. They didn't appreciate Indigenous cultures and the different family relationships.

Poor housing

Living on the reserve required many adjustments. Traditionally, Indigenous Peoples lived on a large land base and were free to move across the land to hunt and gather food. They could provide for their families and communities. On reserves, they were restricted to small and often remote plots of land that made living well much more difficult.

This photo from 1958 shows the small family cabin of Mr. and Mrs. Hebron Roulette and their two children on the Sandy Bay Reserve in Manitoba.

Advocated for better housing

Many First Nations communities advocated for better housing, power and water on reserves. They wanted the same living conditions as other Canadians.

In the 1950s, the government created programs to improve housing conditions on reserves. Indigenous Peoples adapted to the new colonial-style homes.

The Roulette family is shown here in their new home on the Sandy Bay Reserve in Manitoba.

Judging a lifestyle

This photo was taken in 1965 on the Red Earth Reserve in Saskatchewan, part of Treaty 5. Here, a nurse is checking a mother and new baby. Some non-Indigenous workers viewed these living conditions as poor and inadequate, without trying to understand the culture and lifestyle. Children were often removed for the crime of poverty.

Church is in charge

Indigenous Peoples were often the target of Christian-run organizations who saw them as groups deserving of charity and in need of spiritual and moral guidance. Having access to Indigenous children through health care, education and social programs made it easy for a church to intervene and remove even the youngest babies from their parents.

Page 1

GOVERNMENT OF THE PROVINCE OF ALBERTA

HSD 16

DEPARTMENT OF HEALTH AND SOCIAL DEVELOPMENT

Social and Family History

NOTE: Workers should note very carefully Policy Manual, Child Welfare 13, for instructions regarding completion and submission of this form.

SECTION 1 - Report of Child Protection Intake

1.   Date report received by DHSD: _____

2.(c) Departmental file number (if not known, list as N/K): _____

3.(c) Regional office receiving report: _____

4.(c) Report received concerning:

	Name	Address	Telephone
Biological		"SEC. 5"	
(a) Father		"SEC. 5"	
(b) Mother			

Intake form

After the Indian Act was amended in 1951, provincial child welfare agencies began to intervene in Indigenous families on-reserve. Soon, Indigenous communities were struggling against a wave of child welfare interventions that removed their children from the home for the purpose of placing them in foster care.

This is a typical child protection intake form used to record information about a child entering care from the Alberta Department of Health and Social Development.

HOMES NEEDED FOR 47

Adoption Prospects Are Slim When Children Are Not 'White'

By NOEL SWANN

Racist attitudes

The Government of Canada and child welfare agencies were prejudiced against Indigenous families. This is reflected in their aggressive removal of children to residential schools and later to foster care. The Canadian public also harboured racist attitudes. As this 1960s *Winnipeg Free Press* article claims, "Adoption prospects slim when children are not white."

One longtime employee of the Ministry of Human Resources in B.C. referred to [the] process as the "Sixties Scoop." She admitted that provincial social workers would, quite literally, scoop children from reserves on the slightest pretext. She also made it clear, however, that she and her colleagues sincerely believed that what they were doing was in the best interests of the children. They felt that the apprehension of Indian children from reserves would save them from the effects of crushing poverty, unsanitary health conditions, poor housing and malnutrition, which were facts of life on many reserves. Unfortunately, the long-term effect of apprehension on the individual child was not considered. More likely, it could not have been imagined. Nor were the effects of apprehension on Indian families and communities taken in account and some reserves lost almost a generation of their children as a result.

— Excerpt from interview with British Columbia government employee

RCMP involvement

RCMP officers, like the one pictured here in red serge, were used to apprehend children for residential schools. They also often accompanied social workers during child apprehensions in case parents tried to resist.

The Children Are Taken

At the core of the Sixties Scoop was the belief that Indigenous children were better off with white families. Governments, social workers, health professionals, the clergy and the RCMP were all part of a system designed to separate Indigenous children from their parents. The Adopt Indian and Métis program, known as AIM, was a prime example of this. Indigenous children were sent out of province and out of country. But there was resistance. By the early 1970s, Métis activists like Phyllis Trotchie, Nora Thibodeau and Vicki Racette were writing articles, organizing and raising awareness about the removal of children from their communities. They fought to establish their own recognized child welfare system that would not be so quick to remove Indigenous children from the home.

AIM program
The Adopt Indian and Métis program, later called AIM, was launched in 1967. Otto Driedger, seen here in 1969, was the director of child welfare at the Saskatchewan Department of Social Welfare. He was one of the architects of the AIM program. Through this program, Saskatchewan's Department of Social Welfare sought non-Indigenous families in the province to encourage them to adopt Indigenous children. They advertised Indigenous children through multiple media — on television, in the newspaper and on the radio.

Some parents resisted
Child apprehensions were not necessarily a simple matter. When Indigenous parents resisted, they were threatened with arrest. Some parents disappeared into "the bush" to hide their children when Indian Agents, the RCMP or social workers came around, but this was not always possible. Parents fought the system, but success was very hard to come by.

GWEN

Gwen is a beautiful little girl with a deceptively sad looking appearance, now 2¾ years old. While she is wary of strangers she does like lots of love and cuddling. She is independent and can readily amuse herslf. Gwen works off lots of energy riding her tricycle. She gets along well with playmates.

· While Gwen enjoys general good health, her left foot is affected by cerebral palsy which causes her to walk with a slight limp and to wear a leg brace below the knee. This condition will not deteriorate. When she is 4 years old she will have a "tendon transfer" operation which will strengthen her foot. She will then continue to wear the brace until she is about 13 years of age at which time she will have a second operation to perform bone surgery on her heel. After that, it is expected that she will be able to go brace free.

Parents wishing to discuss the adoption of Gwen may contact:

Aim Centre

2340 Albert Street	Room 210, 1030 Idylwyld Dr. N.
REGINA, Saskatchewan	SASKATOON, Saskatchewan
S4P 2V7	S7L 4J7
Phone: 523-6681	Phone: 653-2056

AIM ads

AIM ads like these were placed in newspapers. The ads had more in common with pet adoptions than with children. Indigenous children taken into foster care were undergoing some of the most challenging experiences of their life. Yet the descriptions in the ads do not reflect any respect for the child, their challenges or their privacy.

 Watch the video at https://tinyurl.com/CBC-News-on-AIM-1968

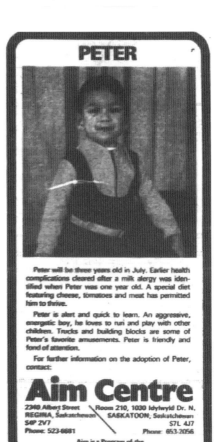

PETER

Peter will be three years old in July. Earlier health complications cleared after a milk allergy was identified when Peter was one year old. A special diet featuring cheese, tomatoes and meat has permitted him to thrive.

Peter is alert and quick to learn. An aggressive, energetic boy, he loves to run and play with other children. Trucks and building blocks are some of Peter's favorite amusements. Peter is friendly and fond of attention.

For further information on the adoption of Peter, contact:

Aim Centre

2340 Albert Street	Room 210, 1030 Idylwyld Dr. N.
REGINA, Saskatchewan	SASKATOON, Saskatchewan
S4P 2V7	S7L 4J7
Phone: 523-6681	Phone: 653-2056

Aim is a Program of the Saskatchewan Department of Social Services

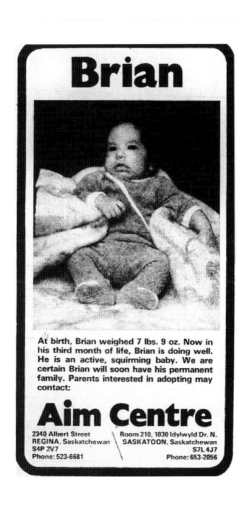

Brian

At birth, Brian weighed 7 lbs. 9 oz. Now in his third month of life, Brian is doing well. He is an active, squirming baby. We are certain Brian will soon have his permanent family. Parents interested in adopting may contact:

Aim Centre

2340 Albert Street	Room 210, 1030 Idylwyld Dr. N.
REGINA, Saskatchewan	SASKATOON, Saskatchewan
S4P 2V7	S7L 4J7
Phone: 523-6681	Phone: 653-2056

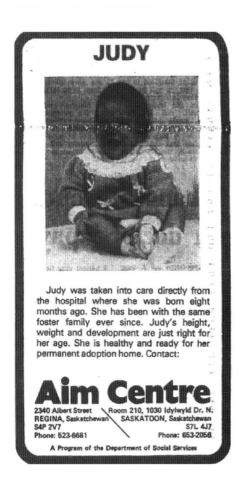

JUDY

Judy was taken into care directly from the hospital where she was born eight months ago. She has been with the same foster family ever since. Judy's height, weight and development are just right for her age. She is healthy and ready for her permanent adoption home. Contact:

Aim Centre

2340 Albert Street	Room 210, 1030 Idylwyld Dr. N.
REGINA, Saskatchewan	SASKATOON, Saskatchewan
S4P 2V7	S7L 4J7
Phone: 523-6681	Phone: 653-2056

A Program of the Department of Social Services

The Children Are Taken

The Scoop
This 2018 painting, *The Scoop* by Kent Monkman, depicts the brutal removal of children from their homes by church and state officials.

Salesperson of the year
This disturbing office memo reflects the attitudes of staff in the AIM program. It announces the Saskatchewan Department of Social Welfare's "Salesperson of the Year" award in 1973. The award was presented to the person who placed the most Indigenous children as permanent wards with non-Indigenous families.

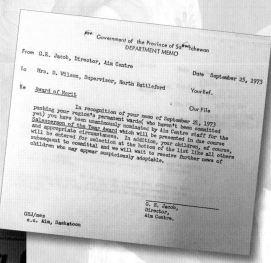

Seeking foster families
The headline reads, "Brown-skinned babies, too, need loving." AIM ads like these were piloted from 1967 to 1969 and were deemed a success. They continued until the early 1970s.

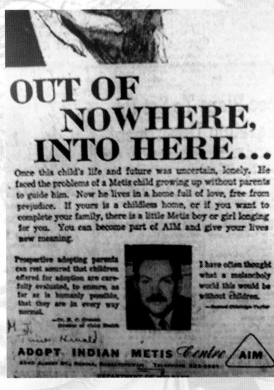

Anti-AIM ad

Deeply disturbed by both the AIM advertisements and the government efforts at transracial adoptions for Indigenous children, many Indigenous people fought back. The Métis Foster Home Committee was organized against AIM ads and the AIM program. It developed a Métis foster home program that would take control of the foster program. "We object to Métis children being shipped out of the province of Saskatchewan for adoption to white homes in other provinces." This was part of larger efforts to push back against the taking of Indigenous children into provincial child welfare programs. This is an anti-AIM advertisement, calling out Canada for having segregated adoption centres.

Out of nowhere?
Ads like this one made it appear as if Indigenous children were without parents, community or cultural connections of any kind. As if the children came from "out of nowhere."

WATCH THE VIDEO

Watch the video at
https://tinyurl.com/CBC-News-on-AIM-1971

"Once this child's life and future was uncertain, lonely. He faced the problems of a Métis child, growing up without parents to guide him. Now he lives in a home full of love, free from prejudice. If yours is a childless home, or if you want to complete a family, there is a little Métis boy or girl looking for you. You can become part of AIM and give your lives new meaning. Prospective adopting parents can rest assured that children offered for adoption are carefully evaluated, to assure, as far as is humanly possible, that they are in every way normal." — AIM Advertisement

Where Were Children Taken?

The Government of Canada aggressively pursued its colonial agenda. Over decades, social workers across the country took Indigenous children from their homes and placed them with primarily white families. Children were moved all over the world. Most lost their language, culture and identity.

Kids came from across Canada

Indigenous children in Canadian provinces and territories were taken from their homes and sent all over Canada, often outside of their home province. Some were also taken outside of the country. Many went to the United States and some went overseas. This map is based on Survivor reporting and may not be complete.

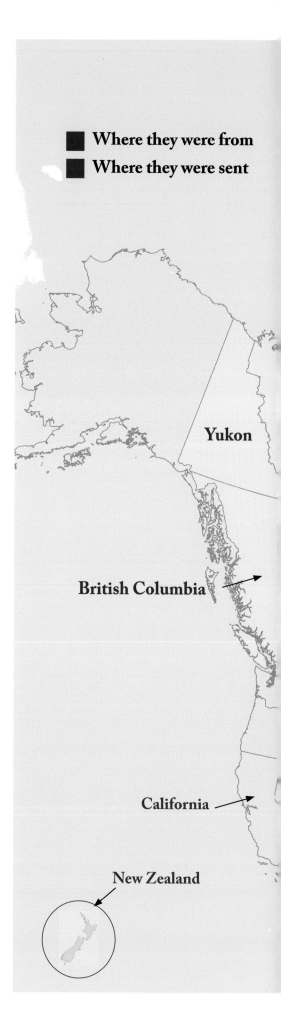

■ **Where they were from**
■ **Where they were sent**

Yukon

British Columbia

California

New Zealand

The Sixties Scoop (1951–1985)

The Netherlands

United
Kingdom

Germany

Nunavut

Northwest
Territories

CANADA

Manitoba

Newfoundland

Alberta

Quebec

Saskatchewan

Ontario

Nova Scotia

Minnesota

Massachusetts

New York

Michigan

Pennsylvania

India

Maryland

UNITED STATES

Botswana

Survivors' Stories

By its end, the Sixties Scoop took over 20,000 Indigenous children from their homes and deliberately placed them outside of their communities, usually with white families. Many Survivors speak of the trauma they endured, but not all Survivors had horrible experiences. Some foster placements were bad and others were not. Many children were placed in more than one foster home so they may have had a range of experiences.

Indigenous Peoples are strong, and most stories of Sixties Scoop survival contain elements of healing and recovery, too. This healing is often done through reclaiming their cultures and their Indigenous heritage. These brave people have told their stories to help us all understand the impact of the Sixties Scoop.

Grew up on a farm
Adam North Peigan and his foster parent Johnny Walter Zobell. Adam was twelve years old the first time he met his birth mother. As an adult (right) Adam is the president of the Legacy of Hope Foundation board.

Taken as an infant
Adam North Peigan was removed from his family when he was very young.

WATCH THE VIDEO

Watch the video at
https://tinyurl.com/LHF-Adam-North-Peigan

"A lot of people don't really remember, don't even know what happened to them. But what I've been told is that I was actually an infant when I was removed from my community of the Piikani First Nation in Southern Alberta. All my brothers and sisters were fostered out. I was apprehended by Alberta's Social Services Child Welfare, I was removed, and I was placed in non-Indigenous foster homes. Right up until the age of seventeen. My foster mother, I remember, I was four years old, and my foster mother . . . used to throw me in the tub and tell me that I was dirty because of my skin. Today I can say that I am very proud to be a First Nations person. I am very proud to be Blackfoot. And it's a really really good feeling to be able to be proud of who you are. I've gone back to my community. I've worked in my community. I've been there. I've actually served in leadership in my community."

— Adam North Peigan

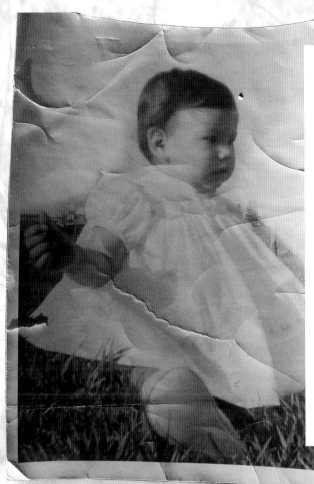

Endured many challenges
Angela Ashawasegai, pictured in these childhood photos, is a member of the Henvey Inlet First Nation, Ontario. After being taken in the Sixties Scoop, she endured many years of difficulty at the hands of others.

Healed herself
After struggling for several years, Angela Ashawasegai, seen here, graduated from university and pursued spiritual teachings to heal herself from the trauma she endured in the child welfare system. She now provides Indigenous spiritual therapy treatment for others to help them heal.

Reconnecting with culture
Angela does beading as part of reconnecting to her culture. She created this circular floral beadwork picture. Many Survivors lost their cultural connections and have had to re-learn lost skills or learn them for the first time. Many find healing through traditional arts.

Brothers separated

Eric Stewart is Nisga'a. He and his brother Patrick were taken from their family when very young and separated into different foster homes. Eric endured incredible hardships and trauma. Their biological grandfather fought to get them home so he could care for them. Authorities said, "No." Eric recalled, "He would come to Vancouver and demand that us boys be returned to him. He would say, 'I don't want money, I have a big house, and of course, they said no . . .'"

Mother survived residential school

Patrick is Eric Stewart's brother. Patrick and Eric's mother was a residential school Survivor. She had endured trauma at residential school and found it difficult to be a parent. Instead of helping her, social services took her children away.

Parents searched for them

Sharon Gladue-Paskimin, pictured here as a child, was adopted into a non-Indigenous family with her sister when they were very young. "To my parents we did no wrong. I remember there was a lot of laughter. There were experiences of going out trapping and hunting with them . . . visiting with other families . . . And I always remember it was a good loving, nurturing home. I was about two when I was taken for the very first time . . . Prior to being fostered out, my mom told us that we never spoke a word of English. We were fluent in Cree." Sharon's parents were devastated when she and her sister were taken away. "My parents would hitchhike to different communities, looking for us."

"To my parents we did no wrong. I remember there was a lot of laughter. There were experiences of going out trapping and hunting with them, swimming behind the house, and visiting with other families as well too. And I always remember it was a good loving, nurturing home. I was about two when I was taken for the very first time. I don't have a recollection of how many homes, but I do remember over five homes, and finally adopted out in Delisle, Saskatchewan. My parents would hitchhike to different communities, looking for us. They would hear rumours that there was two little native girls living in the community . . . So, they would hitchhike to communities and they would look for us, but to no avail."

— Sharon Gladue-Paskimin

WATCH THE VIDEO

Watch the video at
https://tinyurl.com/LHF-Sharon-Gladue

Traditional kinship

This photo shows Anishinaabe families living together at a campground in Kenora, Ontario. When Indigenous families lived in their traditional kinship relationships, the children did well. Adults shared the duties of raising children. But often non-Indigenous social workers didn't understand this shared role. Because it was different than their own experience, they viewed it as a problem that Indigenous children had to be rescued from and they sought to remove them from their homes.

Lost their language

Before they were taken from their parents, Sharon Gladue-Paskimin and her sister lived in their Cree community in Saskatchewan. This young Cree girl and her mother were photographed in 1969, in North Battleford, Saskatchewan, where Sharon lived as a foster child. Placed in mostly white foster homes, many children lost their connection to their language and rich cultural traditions.

"Prior to being fostered out, my mom told us that we never spoke a word of English. We were very very fluent in Cree."

— Sharon Gladue-Paskimin

Became a social worker

Sharon Gladue-Paskimin is pictured here as an adult. Sharon's experiences as a child in the system eventually led her to become a social worker herself. "I always swore that I was never gonna be a social worker, but I went back and I got my Aboriginal Child and Family Services diploma. And with that education and all the grief and trauma training that I received, I was able to move forward and start advocating and helping families." Sharon is the former vice president of the Sixties Scoop Indigenous Society of Alberta.

"My foster homes were quite abusive. It was just a lot of emotional and psychological and cultural abuse. My adopted dad was one of the kindest most gentlest men you will ever come across. He had the twinkle in the eye when he smiled. He always protected us. But because of the hours that he worked, very rare was he home. Meanwhile, on the other hand, my adopted mother, she was very abusive. We were always scared, always frightened."

— Sharon Gladue-Paskimin

Survivors' Stories

Poet and activist

Maya Cousineau Mollen, pictured here, has become a poet and an activist for Indigenous rights. Her experiences and perspective have fueled her work in different organizations trying to change how Canada sees and treats Indigenous Peoples. She has worked on the Inquiry into Missing and Murdered Indigenous Women and Girls and is a founding board member for the Sixties Scoop Healing Foundation. In 2022, Maya became the Indigenous Writer in Residence at McGill University. Maya writes poetry, mostly in French. She explores themes and issues from both of her family backgrounds — French and Indigenous.

Two cultures

Maya Cousineau Mollen was born to an Innu family in Ekuanitshit, Quebec. She was removed from her family and adopted by a white family in Quebec. Her adopted parents and her biological parents knew each other. Because of this, Maya was able to learn about both of her cultural backgrounds as she grew up. Maya is pictured here as a young girl with her birth mother.

Loss of culture

This image shows an Inuit family drumming in 1950 in the Padlei region of the Northwest Territories. Maya Cousineau Mollen was able to maintain contact with her birth parents and culture, but many others suffered the loss of culture and language, music, teachings and knowledge, the safety of family and community.

First Powwow

Sixties Scoop Survivor Christin Dennis recalls below what it was like to reconnect with his culture. This image was taken on the Kainai Reserve, Alberta, in 1953 during their summer celebrations. The young dancer is in full ceremonial regalia, ready to perform the sacred steps of the sun dance in time to the beating drums and ceremonial songs.

> "When I first went to my first Powwow, I was so enthralled, and it was just so beautiful because I didn't know how to dance, but it was almost like when I was there it was like a celebration of ourselves. Like we were celebrating who we were. And I remember I just like, I felt so proud in that moment to be who I was."
>
> — Christin Dennis

Lived with shame and guilt

Christin Dennis holds a photo from his childhood. He recounts how he had a children's bow since he was little that he would carry with his medicines.

WATCH THE VIDEO

Watch the video at
https://tinyurl.com/Christin-Dennis

Sitting Bull

Christin Dennis was greatly influenced by a book he read about the famous Lakota warrior Sitting Bull, photographed here in 1885. "I found a book in the archives about Sitting Bull. And I read that book and I was so appalled by what happened to our people . . . I found myself." He began to turn his life around and take part in sweat lodges to help with his healing.

> "When I was taken from my birth family, I believe I was two years old. There was a lot of abuse in that family. I used to live with a lot of shame and guilt with them — the sister would always say 'I wish we never adopted you, you're not my brother.' My [foster] brother would beat me up. And I don't understand why he would hit, beat me up, and you know, I'm crying and he would laugh at me. I became an addict. I lived with shame — shame with my family, shame with my people, of who I was . . . The last [foster family] that I was with, they were really wonderful people. They provided, they took me to Powwow . . . I said to my foster father, 'I want a bow.' And he carved me a bow within that week, and that's the bow that I have now."
>
> — Christin Dennis

Inuit traditions

Inuit have a rich tradition of drumming and singing. Drummers, like Ihartataittuq Itirujuk pictured here, might perform for special occasions, like a birth or marriage, to mark the passing of a loved one or to celebrate a young boy's first hunt. Tauni Sheldon: "[My son], he's very proud of who he is, he'll drum, he'll dance, he'll throat sing . . . It's got to stop these cycles of trauma so he can be who he is and know he's comfortable, safe, loved and happy."

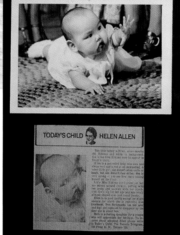

First Inuit baby advertised for adoption

Tauni Sheldon was advertised in *The Toronto Telegram* as the "first Inuit baby advertised for adoption in Toronto." Tauni says. "I can only imagine being a mother and having him taken from me when he was born."

"I was fortunate to go to a good and loving home. I was given opportunity and welcomed into that family, I've always had the freedom to explore my roots and where I come from. I didn't want to be Inuk for the younger years of my life. I was picked on horribly during school . . . For non-Inuit family, there wasn't really a big understanding of truly of what I was going through and how I felt."

— Tauni Sheldon

Reconnecting with Inuit culture

Tauni Sheldon poses with her eleven-year-old son. Tauni was removed from her unwed Inuit mother three hours after she was born. Tauni was raised in a loving home but has spent many years learning and reconnecting with her Inuit culture.

WATCH THE VIDEO

Watch the video at https://tinyurl.com/Tauni-Sheldon

Sisters were separated
Many siblings were separated due to the Sixties Scoop. This is an image of Patricia, Gina and Colleen Hele as children.

Survivor turned activist
Colleen Hele-Cardinal is from Saddle Lake First Nation, Alberta. She is the daughter of a residential school Survivor and she is a Sixties Scoop Survivor. Colleen is a social justice activist and co-founder of the National Indigenous Survivors of Child Welfare Network. She has organized national Indigenous adoptee gatherings.

A troubled life
Carla Harris as a baby.

"I was born in Regina, Saskatchewan. I stayed in the hospital for a bit and then they moved me to a foster home outside in Regina, so my mother couldn't come and get me . . . I was adopted when I was nine months old in a small town in a white community. There had been abuse and I had run away on my fourteenth birthday. I was in several foster homes, group homes, even juvenile detention centres because I was a runaway and they couldn't keep me in any place."

— Carla Harris

Reunited with family
Carla Harris is pictured here holding one of her baby outfits, a rare keepsake for a child in the system who was moved around to so many places. At twenty-one, she made contact with her biological family. "They had actually been looking for me."

CHAPTER 4

Pushing Back (1970s–1985)

AIM and Red Power

Starting in the 1970s, Indigenous Peoples across North America began making headway in their push back against the discriminatory and assimilationist policies of colonial governments. In Canada and the United States, groups like the American Indian Movement (AIM) and the Red Power Movement organized protests and fought for Indigenous rights.

Indigenous groups organized
In the 1970s, Indigenous groups from across North America began to organize and work together. In the United States, the American Indian Movement (AIM) pushed back against unjust colonial policies and practices. This is AIM's flag.

 **WATCH THE VIDEO** ► *Watch the video at https://tinyurl.com/Aim-and-Wounded-Knee*

Women fought too
Dennis Banks, Clyde Bellecourt and Russell Means, pictured here in 1970 at Wounded Knee, are considered AIM's founding members. Women, such as Pat Bellanger, Sarah Bad Heart Bull and Anna Mae Aquash, also joined AIM to fight for their rights. AIM inspired similar movements in Canada.

 **WATCH THE VIDEO** ► *Watch the video at https://tinyurl.com/Who-is-AIM*

"The White Paper" promoted assimilation
In 1969, Jean Chrétien (above), Minister of Indian Affairs and Northern Development, released the "Statement of the Government of Canada on Indian Policy," also known as "The White Paper." It proposed to abolish Indigenous status, treaty rights and responsibilities, and remove Indigenous land rights. It was an attempt to forcefully colonize Indigenous Peoples into Canadian society. The Indigenous community in Canada worked together to stop this from happening.

Increasing awareness of Indigenous issues

Howard Adams was a Métis activist and scholar from Saskatchewan. He wrote about how the Government of Canada and Canadian society treated Indigenous Peoples. In 1995, he published *Tortured People: The Politics of Colonization*. Adams also taught at the University of Saskatchewan. His writings and teachings were important foundations for the Red Power Movement in Canada.

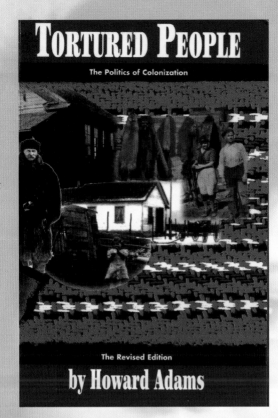

TORTURED PEOPLE
The Politics of Colonization

The Revised Edition

by Howard Adams

Red Paper presentation

Harold Cardinal (centre) was a young, influential Indigenous leader in 1970. Here he is presenting "The Red Paper" to Alberta Premier Harry Strom (left) and Jean Chrétien. Indigenous push back to "The White Paper" was widespread and received a lot of media attention.

A. THE PREAMBLE

To us who are Treaty Indians there is nothing more important than our Treaties, our lands and the well being of our future generation. We have studied carefully the contents of the Government White Paper on Indians and we have concluded that it offers despair instead of hope. Under the guise of land ownership, the government has devised a scheme whereby within a generation or shortly after the proposed Indian Lands Act expires our people would be left with no land and consequently the future generation would be condemned to the despair and ugly spectre of urban poverty in ghettos.

In Alberta, we have told the Federal Minister of Indian Affairs that we do not wish to discuss his White Paper with him until we reach a position where we can bring forth viable alternatives because we know that his paper is wrong and that it will harm our people. We refused to meet him on his White Paper because we have been stung and hurt by his concept of consultation.

In his White Paper, the Minister said, "This review was a response to things said by Indian people at the consultation meetings which began a year ago and culminated in a meeting in Ottawa in April." Yet, what Indians asked for land ownership that would result in Provincial taxation of our reserves? What Indians asked that the Canadian Constitution be changed to remove any reference to Indians or Indian lands? What Indians asked that Treaties be brought to an end? What group of Indians asked that aboriginal rights not be recognized? What group of Indians asked for a Commissioner whose purview would exclude half of the Indian population in Canada? The answer is no Treaty Indians asked for any of these things and yet through his concept of "consultation," the Minister said that his White Paper was in response to things said by Indians.

We felt that with this concept of consultation held by the Minister and his department, that if we met with them to discuss the contents of his White Paper without being fully prepared, that even if we just talked about the weather, he would turn around and tell Parliament and the Canadian public that we accepted his White Paper.

"The Red Paper"

This Citizens Plus document, known as "The Red Paper," was produced by the Indian Association of Alberta in 1970 in response to the federal government's "White Paper." "The Red Paper" outlined a powerful vision of Indigenous rights and sovereignty and how they could be achieved. It was an important tool in the ongoing Red Power Movement.

The Government of Canada backs down

The government was surprised by Indigenous Peoples' response to "The White Paper." Indigenous resistance, including "The Red Paper," caused Prime Minister Pierre Trudeau (left) to drop "The White Paper."

The shocking truth

Maria Campbell, Métis scholar and activist, published her autobiography *Half-Breed* in 1973. She wrote about the racism and sexism Indigenous women experienced at the hands of Canadians. Her shocking story offered more insight into how Indigenous Peoples continued to be treated by many Canadians.

HALF-BREED
THE POWERFUL LIFE STORY OF A WOMAN WHOSE COURAGE AND STRENGTH YOU WILL NEVER FORGET!

MARIA CAMPBELL

Culturally Relevant Care

Up until the late 1970s, provincial child welfare agencies were empowered to take Indigenous children from their communities. Instead of providing Indigenous families with much-needed support, the system was designed to separate Indigenous families. To fight back against this, some First Nations launched their own child welfare agencies. These agencies were very different from their provincial, non-Indigenous counterparts. Instead of taking Indigenous children from their homes and putting them in government care, or adopting them out, Indigenous-led child welfare agencies fought to keep families together. These Indigenous-run agencies used cultural frameworks to guide their work. They also focused on healing relationships and providing support services and resources for families.

Staff are well trained
The staff at an Indigenous-led child welfare agency, such as Kina Gbezhgomi Child and Family Services (pictured here), might include social workers, therapists, counsellors, nurses and community Elders. They understand issues families may be struggling with and offer culturally relevant supports and services.

Indigenous-led child welfare agencies fought to keep families together.

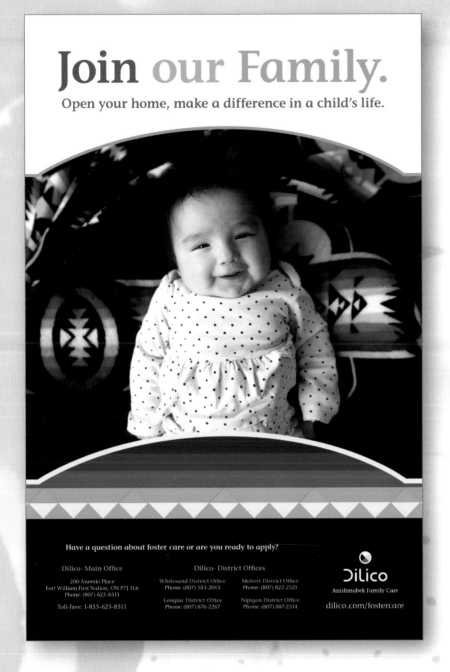

Dilico poster

Indigenous child welfare services are guided by the cultural practices of the community. If children do need to go into foster care, every effort is made to keep children in their communities and connected to their culture. Dilico Anishinabek Family Care Centre in Fort William First Nation, Ontario, was formed in 1986 and has been serving families in the community and surrounding area ever since. Families and children are supported through programs like parenting classes, child abuse prevention strategies, traditional healing with Elders and Knowledge Keepers and counselling services for the whole family to offer the family tools to stay together.

OTHER AGENCIES

The Kimelman Report

The Indigenous community in Manitoba pressured the provincial government to launch an inquiry into provincial child welfare services. In particular, they drew attention to the high numbers of Indigenous children taken out of their communities and put into non-Indigenous foster care homes outside the province, and sometimes outside the country. In 1982, Associate Chief Judge Edwin C. Kimelman was asked to chair the committee and report on Manitoba's child welfare practices with respect to First Nations and Métis. Published in 1985, the official name of the report is *No Quiet Place*, but it is often referred to as the Kimelman Report. Judge Kimelman and the committee concluded that the province's child welfare practices amounted to cultural genocide.

Kimelman Report led to reforms
Judge Kimelman's (pictured here) report led to an increased call for change. As a result, a series of reforms were introduced across Canada to reduce the number of Indigenous children in care and to improve support for children already in the system.

Parents were not supported
Kimelman's report, pictured here, explains, "With the closing of the Residential Schools, rather than providing the resources on reserves to build economic security and providing the services to support responsible parenting, society found it easier and cheaper to remove the children from their homes and apparently fill the market demand for children in Eastern Canada and the United States" (*No Quiet Place*, page 330).

"The Native people speak of
'custom adoption' and wish this
shared child-rearing practice to
be recognized in law. Essentially,
a custom adoption reflects the
communal responsibility for
raising a child."

— Kimelman Report

Social worker visits
The Kimelman Report recommended
training child welfare staff, like this social
worker, in the area of cultural awareness.

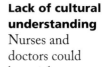

**Lack of cultural
understanding**
Nurses and
doctors could
be quick to
judge a parent's
ability to care for
their children
because they had
different values
around raising
children than
other Canadians,
claiming white
superiority.

"Efforts must be
undertaken to provide
training in the area
of cultural awareness
for those already in
the human service
professions. As far
as can be determined,
professional associations
in the fields of
law, health care,
and social services
have not specifically
provided training for
practitioners, but
cultural issues may be
touched upon in the
course of discussion of
other service delivery
matters."

— Kimelman Report

TRC Calls to Action 1–5

By 1990, some residential school Survivors began to speak publicly about the abuse they had experienced and how it impacted many generations. The Truth and Reconciliation Commission (TRC) was established in 2008 to document the stories of residential school Survivors and to create a plan to guide reconciliation in Canada. After travelling across Canada listening to thousands of Survivors, the commission released "94 Calls to Action" in 2015. The first five dealt specifically with child welfare.

A Child's Dream
In his painting, *A Child's Dream*, Ojibwe artist Isaac Murdoch shows a child spreading hope and happiness to others far away. For children who were taken from their families, their dream of returning helped to sustain them.

Members of the Truth And Reconciliation Commission.
The Truth and Reconciliation Commission (TRC) mission was carried out by Marie Wilson (left), Chief Wilton Littlechild (far right) and Senator (then Chief Justice) Murray Sinclair (second from right). They are pictured here with honourary witness, Renée Dupuis, at the Quebec National Event in April 2013. Their work resulted in essential reports on residential schools. These reports documented how residential schools became early child welfare holding places, setting the stage for the Sixties Scoop.

"The monster that was created in the residential schools moved into a new house. And that monster now lives in the child welfare system."

— Senator Murray Sinclair

Murray Sinclair, chairman of the TRC
The final report of the Truth and Reconciliation Commission containing ninety-four calls to action was released in 2015. It contains essential actions in several areas such as child welfare, education, justice, health, language and culture. These calls to action are meant to be carried out by governments, institutions, churches and Canadian citizens on our path to reconciliation with Indigenous Peoples in Canada.

Bentwood box
This is the bentwood box that the TRC asked Indigenous artist Luke Marston to create. It has symbols representing First Nations, Inuit and Métis communities from across Canada. This sacred box is carved in the traditional method and is made from a single piece of old-growth red cedar. "People placed personal items into the box to symbolize their journey toward healing and expressions of reconciliation."

TRC Recommendation No. 1

"We call upon the federal, provincial, territorial, and Aboriginal governments to commit to reducing the number of Aboriginal children in care."

- 1/94

cbc.ca/unreserved

Call to Action #1
The TRC calls to action begin by addressing the number of Indigenous children in child welfare services. The goal is to reduce the number of Indigenous children in care.

> We call upon the federal, provincial, territorial, and Aboriginal governments, to commit to reducing the number of Aboriginal children in care by:

i. Monitoring and assessing neglect investigations.

ii. Providing adequate resources to enable Aboriginal communities and child-welfare organizations to keep Aboriginal families together where it is safe to do so, and to keep children in culturally appropriate environments, regardless of where they reside.

iii. Ensuring that social workers and others who conduct child-welfare investigations are properly educated and trained about the history and impacts of residential schools.

iv. Ensuring that social workers and others who conduct child-welfare investigations are properly educated and trained about the potential for Aboriginal communities and families to provide more appropriate solutions to family healing.

v. Requiring that all child-welfare decision makers consider the impact of the residential school experience on children and their caregivers.

Truth and
Reconciliation
Commission of Canada
The First Call to Action

> We call upon the federal government, in collaboration with the provinces and territories, to prepare and publish annual reports on the number of Aboriginal children (First Nations, Inuit, and Métis) who are in care, compared with non-Aboriginal children, as well as the reasons for apprehension, the total spending on preventive and care services by child-welfare agencies, and the effectiveness of various interventions.

Truth and
Reconciliation
Commission of Canada
The Second Call to Action

" We call upon all levels of government to fully implement Jordan's Principle. "

Truth and
Reconciliation
Commission of Canada
The Third Call to Action

" We call upon the federal government to enact Aboriginal child-welfare legislation that establishes national standards for Aboriginal child apprehension and custody cases and includes principles that:

i. Affirm the right of Aboriginal governments to establish and maintain their own child-welfare agencies.

ii. Require all child-welfare agencies and courts to take the residential school legacy into account in their decision making.

iii. Establish, as an important priority, a requirement that placements of Aboriginal children into temporary and permanent care be culturally appropriate. "

Truth and
Reconciliation
Commission of Canada
The Fourth Call to Action

" We call upon the federal, provincial, territorial, and Aboriginal governments, to develop culturally appropriate parenting programs for Aboriginal families. "

Truth and
Reconciliation
Commission of Canada
The Fifth Call to Action

The work of reconciliation begins
Prime Minister Justin Trudeau is pictured here addressing the members of the TRC on December 15, 2015, at the release of its final report. This was an important ceremony and many Indigenous leaders, Survivors and politicians attended. All political parties in Canada bear responsibility to see the calls to action carried out.

Provincial Apologies

Before the Sixties Scoop settlement was finalized, three provinces made public apologies for the part they played in the removal of thousands of Indigenous children from their communities. These provincial apologies were written in consultation with Survivors and are important steps toward reconciliation. As of 2023, only Alberta, Manitoba and Saskatchewan had apologized. It is important to note that the Sixties Scoop occurred in every province and territory in Canada (except Nunavut, which was part of the Northwest Territories until 1999). There is much work to be done to recognize, apologize for and reckon with this history. The Ontario Association of Children's Aid Societies has also apologized for their role in the Sixties Scoop. The federal government has not issued a national apology, something many Survivors would like to see happen.

Crowds came to hear the apology
In June 2015, the Province of Manitoba was the first in Canada to apologize. Then-premier Greg Selinger is pictured here.

Official Manitoba apology

This is an excerpt from the official apology:

"I would like to apologize on behalf of the Province of Manitoba for the '60s Scoop — the practice of removing First Nation, Métis and Inuit children from their families and placing them for adoption in non-Indigenous homes, sometimes far from their home community, and for the losses of culture and identity to the children and their families and communities . . . With these words of apology and regret, I hope that all Canadians will join me in recognizing this historical injustice."

MINISTERIAL STATEMENTS
APOLOGY TO FIRST NATION, MÉTIS AND INUIT SURVIVORS OF THE SIXTIES SCOOP

INTRODUCTION

Thank you Mr. Speaker, before I begin my statement, I'd like to provide the requisite copies to the Legislature.

Mr. Speaker, elders, survivors, guests, and members of this chamber, I am humbled today to speak about a tragedy widely known as the "Sixties Scoop". This wide-scale, national apprehension of Indigenous children by child-welfare agencies removed thousands of children from their families and communities.

Je me présente avec humilité aujourd'hui pour parler de la tragédie connue sous le nom "Sixties Scoop". Cette appréhension à échelle nationale d'enfants autochtones par notre système social a enlevé des milliers d'enfants de leur familles et de leur communautés.

These children were placed in Non-Aboriginal homes across Canada, the United States and even overseas. While some adoptive families took steps to provide culturally appropriate supports to adopted children, the Sixties Scoop is recognized as a practice of forced assimilation, and one that extended well beyond the 1960s.

LEGACY OF THE SIXTIES SCOOP

There is not an Indigenous person in this country who has not been affected by the residential schools legacy, and the number of Indigenous people affected by the Sixties Scoop is also very large.

Across Canada, the number of adoptees is estimated to exceed 20,000 First Nation, Métis and Inuit children. By separating these children from their families, they were stripped of their culture, language and traditions.

Judge Edwin Kimelman the author of the 1985 report "No Quiet Place" on the child welfare system and how it affected Aboriginal people described the Sixties Scoop practice as "cultural genocide" – the very term that Chief Justice Beverley McLachlin and Commissioner Murray Sinclair used to describe the residential schools system. It is important that we acknowledge and appreciate the meaning of that description.

1

Premier Selinger apologizes

In June 2015, the Province of Manitoba was the first in Canada to apologize to Indigenous Peoples for its role in the Sixties Scoop. This is Premier Greg Selinger delivering the apology in the Manitoba legislature.

Watch the video at
https://tinyurl.com/Manitoba-Apologizes

Apology

We the Ontario Association of Children's Aid Societies and the non-Indigenous Children's Aid Societies of Ontario apologize to Indigenous families, children, and communities for our role in the Sixties Scoop and our continued role in the present day over-representation of Indigenous children in our system.

We acknowledge that we, as the Children's Aid Societies, were aware of or should have been aware of the damage and trauma created first by residential schools, then carried forward by our participation in the Sixties Scoop. We saw the broken and devastated communities and were complacent in the belief that the fault was all yours. It was not. The actions we participated in clearly led you to this point.

We apologize to the children, mothers, and fathers who have been hurt by the Sixties Scoop, and who currently find themselves caught up in the child welfare system. During the Sixties Scoop child welfare agencies removed thousands of Indigenous children from their homes, families, and communities across Canada. Many of these children were placed in non-Indigenous homes across Canada, the United States, and even overseas. While some adoptive families did their best to love and care for the Indigenous children, the Sixties Scoop is now recognized as a practice of forced assimilation—one that extended well beyond the 1960s and into the 1980s.

Justice Edwin Kimmelman, the author of the 1985 report **No Quiet Place** on the child welfare system and how it affected Indigenous people, described the practice of the Sixties Scoop as "cultural genocide." This is the same description used by Chief Justice Beverley McLachlin and Commissioner Murray Sinclair to describe the residential school system. While we are working to change this trajectory, we must recognize that today things are worse. Indigenous children continue to be over-represented in our system. They continue to be placed in homes and institutions far from their families and communities. Even in 2017, these placements are not culturally safe. The children tell us this in their words and through their actions of suicide and self-harm.

We have not adequately addressed the need for healing from trauma that is essential for Indigenous communities to move forward. We do not have the proper distribution of resources such that Indigenous organizations are providing the child welfare services to their children and such that treatment opportunities are readily available so that healing can happen closer to home.

It is important that we acknowledge and appreciate the impact and meaning of cultural genocide to the Indigenous people of Ontario. The Sixties Scoop has been a continuation of the inter-generational traumas and cultural loss inflicted on the Indigenous peoples of Ontario. There continues to be a lack of Indigenous culture-based services for children and families, and there continues to be resistance to Indigenous self-determination with respect to the care of their children and families.

These are historic and current day injustices for which we, as Ontario's non-Indigenous Children's Aid Societies, must take responsibility. These are difficult truths, but they are truths we must speak in order to begin the journey towards healing, change, and Reconciliation.

It is time that we do more than offer words. Today we commit to Indigenous communities that we will continue to seek and implement your guidance as we undertake active measures to ensure that we are serving Indigenous children and families in a manner that empowers children, families, and communities.

The Ontario non-Indigenous Children's Aid Societies have unanimously agreed to prioritize Reconciliation with Indigenous communities through the **following key commitments**:

- Reduce the number of Indigenous children in care.
- Reduce the number of legal files involving Indigenous children and families.
- Increase the use of formal customary care agreements.
- Ensure Indigenous representation and involvement at the local Boards of Directors.
- Implement mandatory, regular Indigenous training for staff.
- Embed Jordan's Principle in service practice and the inter-agency protocol.
- In consultation with Indigenous communities, develop a unique agency-based plan to better address the needs of the children and families from those communities.
- Continue to develop relationships between the local agency and the local Indigenous communities.
- Assist those individuals wanting to see their historical files by accessing and providing the information they request.

The measuring and tracking of each of these commitments is being undertaken at a local and provincial level. Agencies are committed to reporting on outcomes in each of these areas.

The Board of Directors of the Ontario Association of Children's Aid Societies has made the following **four key commitments**:

- Shift resources to Indigenous organizations so that they are better able to provide services for and advocate on behalf of Indigenous children, families, and communities.
- Support Indigenous leadership in their quest for self-governance and legislation regarding the care of children within their local communities.
- Support Indigenous autonomy in the development of specific Indigenous services and the child welfare system.
- Support and encourage non-Indigenous agencies to work with local Indigenous communities to ensure that children and families are served in a way that leads to Reconciliation.

The commitments made by the Ontario child welfare sector represent an acknowledgement that it must do better, be held accountable for results, and work in a framework that recognizes and supports Reconciliation with Indigenous communities.

The Sixties Scoop and many current practices have resulted in immeasurable damage to the Indigenous people of Ontario. These words of apology and regret are only an acknowledgement that we must do better. We have a long path towards Reconciliation and healing of these historic injustices. The OACAS and the local Children's Aid Societies are committed to working with all stakeholders to ensure we are moving towards a healthier future.

Ontario Association of Children's Aid Societies

Mary Ballantyne
Chief Executive Officer

October 3, 2017

We must do better.
In October 2017, the Ontario Association of Children's Aid Societies (OACAS) apologized to Survivors of the Sixties Scoop.

"We apologize to the children, mothers and fathers who have been hurt by the Sixties Scoop, which saw thousands of Indigenous children taken from their home, families and communities across Canada.

"The Sixties Scoop and many current practices have resulted in cultural genocide for the Indigenous people of Ontario. The words of apology and regret I share today are an acknowledgement that we must do better. We have a long path towards Reconciliation and healing of these historic injustices."

— Mary Ballantyne

Working together for the apology
On May 28, 2018, Premier Rachel Notley apologized to Sixties Scoop Survivors on behalf of the Alberta government in the legislature. "From me, as Premier of Alberta, from all of us here as the elected representatives of the people of Alberta, and on behalf of the Government of Alberta, we are sorry."

Watch the video at
https://tinyurl.com/Alberta-Apologizes

"The stories that you, the Survivors, shared with us are heartbreaking. These stories transcend generations: children — kids, babies, toddlers, teens — ripped from your families; parents unable to see through the tears as they took your children away from you; grandparents forced aside as your families were destroyed.

"For the loss of families, of stability, of love, we are sorry.

"For the loss of identity, of language and culture, we are sorry.

"For the loneliness, the anger, the confusion, and the frustration, we are sorry.

"For the government practice that left you Indigenous people estranged from your families and your communities and your history, we are sorry.

"For this trauma, this pain, this suffering, alienation, and sadness, we are sorry."

Government of Alberta
Sixties Scoop Apology

On May 28, 2018, Premier Rachel Notley delivered an historic apology to survivors of the Sixties Scoop, their families and communities. The day began with a pipe ceremony and grand entry into the Alberta legislature. Survivors, their families and leaders from Indigenous communities across Alberta gathered to witness Premier Notley offer an apology in the chamber of the legislature. Below is the transcript of the apology:

Premier Rachel Notley:

Thank you, Mr. Speaker.

I'd like to begin by acknowledging that we are gathered here today on the traditional territory of Treaty 6, and I'd also like to acknowledge the Métis people of Alberta who share a very deep connection with this land.

I rise today in the spirit of truth and reconciliation.

Before we begin, I'd like us all to take a moment and just look up.

When we speak about colonialism and its vestiges, when we speak about the need for truth and reconciliation here in Alberta and across Canada, when we speak about healing, we must remember always that we speak about people.

Above us today are survivors of the Sixties Scoop: women and men, children and grandchildren, parents and grandparents, all of them survivors.

As we speak today in their presence, we are mindful that their presence carries with it also a terrible absence; parents lost; children taken; families destroyed; cultures shamed, ignored, and forgotten; by force, a proud way of life taken away.

The decisions that led to that personal trauma: many of those decisions, Mr. Speaker, were made right here on this floor in this Chamber.

The Government of Alberta owes these people an apology, and today that's what we are here to do.

But for that apology to have the meaning that these women and men deserve, these women and men deserve to know that their experiences were heard and are heard and are understood as best we can.

These women and men deserve to know that we stand here today looking up at them not only with hearts of reconciliation but with eyes that see the wrongs of the past as clearly as we can.

Alberta.ca/SixtiesScoopApology
Published: May 2018

Alberta

News Release

IMMEDIATE RELEASE
Jan. 7, 2019

Government Relations/Executive Council 19-2280

SIXTIES SCOOP APOLOGY - GOVERNMENT OF SASKATCHEWAN

Elder McArthur, thank you for the prayer.

Elders, survivors, Chiefs, distinguished guests, legislative colleagues, ladies and gentlemen.

Good morning everyone.

Welcome to your legislature.

Welcome to Treaty 4 Territory . . . the traditional lands of the Cree, Saulteaux, Dakota, Nakota and Lakota peoples and the home of the Métis.

And welcome to our Dene friends with us this morning.

Before I begin, I want to recognize members of the Sixties Scoop Indigenous Society of Saskatchewan who are with today.

Honoured guests, thank you so much for your participation in the process that has brought us to this point, on this day.

A process that began more than three years ago, under my predecessor, Premier Brad Wall, who first promised this apology on June 24, 2015.

Friends, we would not be here today if not for your determination, your commitment and your courage.

We are deeply indebted to you.

Ladies and gentlemen, this is an important day in the life of our province.

This is a day for our government to acknowledge with honesty, with humility and with deep regret what happened in Saskatchewan.

The Sixties Scoop refers to a period in Canadian history when Indigenous children were removed from their families and their communities by child welfare services.

Thousands of First Nations, Métis and Inuit children were placed in non-Indigenous foster and adoptive homes in Saskatchewan, and in some cases across Canada and the United States.

Media Services/Media Relations Legislative Building, Regina, Canada, S4S 0B3 306-787-6281 www.gov.sk.ca

Official Saskatchewan apology

The Government of Saskatchewan admitted failure on January 7, 2019. The Sixties Scoop Indigenous Society of Saskatchewan (SSISS), in partnership with the government, held sharing circles in six communities — Meadow Lake, North Battleford, Prince Albert, Saskatoon, Fort Qu'Appelle and Regina. More than two hundred Survivors participated in the sharing circles or made submissions online over a three-year period. "I waited fifty-six years for this apology," Sixties Scoop Survivor Robert Doucette said. "I heard the premier say he was sorry, and there was acknowledgment of the harms that they perpetrated on First Nations and Métis children and I appreciate that."

Watch the video at
https://tinyurl.com/Apology-Reaction

"We failed the Survivors we heard from in the sharing circles, and so many others.

"We failed their families.

"We failed their communities.

"We failed.

"On behalf of the Government of Saskatchewan . . . on behalf of the people of Saskatchewan . . . I stand before you today to apologize . . . to say sorry.

"We are sorry for the pain and sadness you experienced.

"We are sorry for the loss of culture and language.

"To all those who lost contact with their family, we are so sorry.

"There is nothing we can offer that will fully restore what you have lost."

— Official Saskatchewan apology

Premier Scott Moe apologizes
In January 2019, Premier Scott Moe, pictured here, delivered the Saskatchewan government's apology to Sixties Scoop Survivors.

Sixties Scoop Settlement

Survivors of the Sixties Scoop, many of whom were the children of residential school Survivors, began to come forward and speak up about their experiences. In 2009, Chief Marcia Brown Martel filed a class action lawsuit in Ontario on behalf of Indigenous children affected by the Sixties Scoop. Over the years, more people joined the lawsuit. In 2017, the Government of Canada agreed to the Sixties Scoop settlement to compensate status First Nations and Inuit for the harm done when they were taken from their families between 1951–1991.

Chief Martel launched a lawsuit

Chief Marcia Brown Martel was taken from her family when she was four years old. In 2009, she became the main plaintiff in a class action lawsuit in Ontario on behalf of Sixties Scoop Survivors. Similar lawsuits were filed against other provincial governments, too.

Awareness and support grew

Support for the lawsuit grew as more people learned about the Sixties Scoop and the abuse that many Indigenous children suffered while in care.

Online support groups

Survivors joined together in online support groups and shared their stories. These young women are raising public awareness of the issues around the Sixties Scoop.

Brown v. Canada (Attorney General) 2017 ONSC 251
COURT FILE NO.: CV-09-372025-CP
DATE: 20170214

SUPERIOR COURT OF JUSTICE – ONTARIO

RE: Marcia Brown / Representative Plaintiff

AND:

The Attorney General of Canada / Defendant

Proceeding under the *Class Proceedings Act, 1992*

BEFORE: Justice Edward P. Belobaba

COUNSEL: *Jeffery Wilson, Morris Cooper* and *Jessica Braude* for the Plaintiff

Owen Young and Gail Sinclair for the Defendant

HEARD: August 23, December 1 and 2, 2016 and written submissions

The "Sixties Scoop"

SUMMARY JUDGMENT ON THE COMMON ISSUE

[1]   After eight years of protracted procedural litigation,[1] the Sixties Scoop class action is before the court for a decision on the first stage of the merits. The representative

---

[1] *Brown v. Canada (Attorney General)* was certified as a class proceeding by Perell J. at 2010 ONSC 3095. Two appeals followed, first to the Divisional Court at 2011 ONSC 7712 and then to the Court of Appeal at 2013 ONCA 18. The Court of Appeal reversed the certification decision and directed that the matter be reheard by a different class action judge. I reheard the matter and again certified the action as a class proceeding at 2013 ONSC 5637. The defendant sought and was granted leave to appeal from my decision at 2014 ONSC 1583. The Divisional Court dismissed the appeal and affirmed the certification at 2014 ONSC 6967.

The pan-Canadian settlement
Chief Marcia Brown Martel sang and drummed on Parliament Hill in October 2017, as she awaited the Pan-Canadian Settlement Agreement to be announced.

'Mixed feelings' over Canada's '60s Scoop' settlement

Ottawa agrees to pay $600m to 16,000 indigenous survivors of its controversial forced adoption programme.

WATCH THE VIDEO

Watch the video at https://tinyurl.com/Scoop-Settlement-Reaction

Mixed reaction to the settlement agreement

The Sixties Scoop Settlement Agreement was controversial. Many Survivors disagreed with who was eligible and how the money would be allocated. For example, Métis and non-status First Nations were completely excluded. This headline came from *Al Jazeera*, October 11, 2017.

Settlement agreement announced

The fight to have their case heard in court took many years. Survivors and their supporters called attention to these hearings and often gathered outside the courthouse to honour and bear witness to the proceedings. The settlement agreement was announced by Carolyn Bennett, Minister of Indigenous-Crown Relations at the time, pictured here.

The Sixties Scoop Settlement Journey

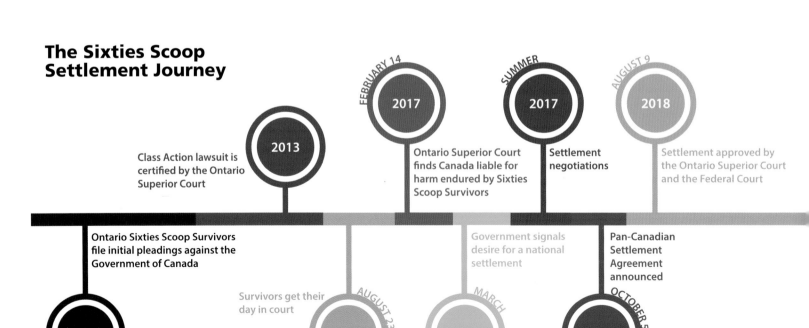

2013 — Class Action lawsuit is certified by the Ontario Superior Court

FEBRUARY 14, 2017 — Ontario Superior Court finds Canada liable for harm endured by Sixties Scoop Survivors

SUMMER 2017 — Settlement negotiations

AUGUST 9, 2018 — Settlement approved by the Ontario Superior Court and the Federal Court

2009 — Ontario Sixties Scoop Survivors file initial pleadings against the Government of Canada

AUGUST 23, 2016 — Survivors get their day in court

MARCH 2017 — Government signals desire for a national settlement

OCTOBER 5, 2017 — Pan-Canadian Settlement Agreement announced

Ottawa agrees to pay $800M to Indigenous victims of '60s Scoop

By **Colin Perkel** The Canadian Press
Thu., Oct. 5, 2017 | 3 min. read

Allocation of settlement money
The $800 million in the settlement was allocated as follows: $75 million for legal fees, $50 million to create the Sixties Scoop Healing Foundation and payments between $25,000 to $50,000 for individual Survivors.

Métis and non-status First Nations were completely excluded from the settlement agreement.

Appeals delay payments
Part of the settlement process is to give those who disagree with the decisions a chance to appeal to the courts and ask the judge to reconsider. While appeals were being heard, no one could receive their payments.

Politics

Attempt to appeal '60s Scoop settlement tossed for 'extreme' lack of evidence

f   y   🚢   in   ✉

'We are pleased that the Federal Court of Appeal has cleared away the last impediment to the settlement'

Colin Perkel · The Canadian Press · Posted: Nov 09, 2018 5:32 PM ET | Last Updated: November 9, 2018

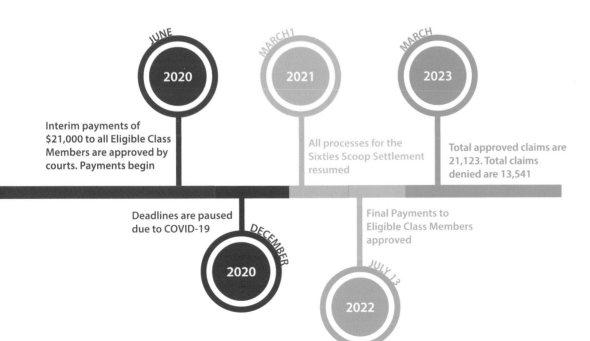

JUNE **2020**
Interim payments of $21,000 to all Eligible Class Members are approved by courts. Payments begin

MARCH 1 **2021**
All processes for the Sixties Scoop Settlement resumed

MARCH **2023**
Total approved claims are 21,123. Total claims denied are 13,541

Deadlines are paused due to COVID-19
DECEMBER **2020**

Final Payments to Eligible Class Members approved
JULY 13 **2022**

Settlement timeline
This timeline breaks down the long legal process of the settlement for Survivors. Some plaintiffs waited more than ten years for justice and a chance to be heard while others died before they saw justice.

Individual Payment Application Form

This is an application form to obtain an individual payment from the Sixties Scoop Settlement Agreement.

The settlement provides a payment to any registered Indian or person eligible to be registered or Inuit person who was adopted or made a permanent ward and was placed in the care of non-Indigenous foster or adoptive parents in Canada between January 1, 1951 and December 31, 1991.

If this describes you, please read and complete the following form. You must then submit it to the Claims Administrator **no later than August 30, 2019** either

(a) by filling out and submitting the electronic version of this form which can be found on the administrator's website at the following address www.sixtiesscoopsettlement.info/ClaimForm

(b) by email, fax or mail, to the following coordinates:

**Sixties Scoop Class Action Administrator
c/o Collectiva Class Action Services, Inc.**
1176 Bishop Street, Suite 208
Montreal, Quebec H3G 2E3
Fax: 514-287-1617
Email: sixtiesscoop@collectiva.ca

For assistance with completing this form you can contact Collectiva at 1-844-287-4270 or by email at sixtiesscoop@collectiva.ca

---

1. What is your full name:
   First name: _____
   Middle name: _____
   Last name: _____

   Have you ever used any other names or legally changed your name?
   (for example: birth names, adopted names, married names, etc.)
   Please list them here: _____
   _____
   _____
   (Please attach copies of legal name change certificates)

   Your current address: _____
   City: _____
   Province: _____
   Postal Code: _____
   Country: _____
   Daytime phone: _____
   Cellular telephone: _____
   Email address: _____

Making a claim could be difficult

This is page one of a form Survivors had to fill out and submit in order to claim any settlement funds. There were a lot of questions and applicants were given a chance to tell their story. In some cases, supporting documents like school or adoption records were required as proof. It could be challenging for some Survivors to obtain these documents. Adoptive parents might not have shared them or kept them.

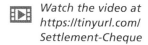

Watch the video at https://tinyurl.com/Settlement-Cheque

Finally, we'd like to provide you with the latest numbers on the administration of the Sixties Scoop Settlement as of June 25, 2020:

- Total number of Individual Payment Applications filed – 34,767
- Total number of Eligible Class Members processed to date – 12,751

For your reference, the breakdown on the administration of the Sixties Scoop Settlement as of May 12, 2020 was:

- Total number of Individual Payment Applications filed – 34,767
- Total number of Eligible Class Members processed to date – 12,551

Many claims were denied

This chart shows the number of claims made to the Sixties Scoop settlement. It took a long time to review and process a claim. Not everyone who applied was eligible for compensation. As of September 2020, over 20,000 claims had been approved, but more than 12,000 had been rejected. It was often very distressing for Survivors whose claims were denied. Some claims were denied due to lack of documentation.

'60s Scoop settlement worth $875M approved by federal judge after Saskatoon hearings

By **Phil Heidenreich** · **Global News**

Posted May 11, 2018 10:54 pm · Updated May 12, 2018 11:00 am

Compensation confirmed

This *Global News* headline from May 2018 confirmed that the Government of Canada was required to compensate Sixties Scoop Survivors.

Money doesn't make up for loss

This June 2020 *CBC* headline refers to Sixties Scoop Survivor, Nina Segalowitz, who was taken from her Fort Smith birth family as part of the Sixties Scoop. "It's not about the money. It's about the time that was lost," she says.

'No amount of money can replace never meeting my mother': Healing an ongoing journey for '60s Scoop survivor

Delivery of interim payments from 2017 settlement expected to start this week

CBC News · Posted: Jun 07, 2020 9:00 AM ADT | Last Updated: June 7, 2020

NEWS | Indigenous | Rights + Justice

'It's Really Cruel': Thousands in Limbo Awaiting '60s Scoop Settlement Money

Nearly 9,700 people are waiting to hear if they're eligible for compensation, 16 months after the application deadline.

Katie Hyslop / 25 Jan 2021 / TheTyee.ca
Katie Hyslop is a reporter for The Tyee. Reach her here.

A slow process

Some applicants waited nearly two years without knowing whether their application had been accepted. The government spokesperson blamed both the pandemic and the need to gather more information from some people for the delay. Some claims were assessed and then re-assessed when new information became available. Claims were reviewed in the order they were received.

Sixties Scoop Survivor Support Groups

The settlement process could be difficult for Survivors. There could be problems obtaining the records needed to file a claim. It might have brought up many painful memories and emotions. The legal process could be confusing and complicated. Organizations like the Legacy of Hope Foundation (LHF), the Sixties Scoop Healing Foundation and the Sixties Scoop Indigenous Society of Alberta (SSISA), helped Survivors as they went through the settlement process. With access to peer support, counselling, legal help, traditional healers and therapists, Survivors were able to get the emotional, mental and legal support they needed during the long process of filing a claim.

Legacy of Hope Foundation
The Legacy of Hope Foundation (LHF) is an Indigenous-led not-for-profit organization founded in 2000. It works across Canada to educate Canadians about the impacts on seven generations of Indigenous children that attended residential/day schools and were forced into the child welfare system. The LHF provides support to Survivors by providing cultural reclamation workshops to help restore cultural pride and community connections. The LHF is guided by the First Nations, Inuit and Métis Survivors who work among the board, staff and project advisory committee.

The path to healing
Richard Kistabish, shown here, highlights the importance of listening to Survivors on their path to healing. "The LHF is guided by the experience and wisdom of residential school and Sixties Scoop Survivors and their families."

Survivors were able to get the emotional, mental and legal support needed to file a claim.

The Sixties Scoop Indigenous Society of Alberta

Adam North Peigan, pictured here in front of an exhibit about the Sixties Scoop, was the president of the Sixties Scoop Indigenous Society of Alberta. The group raised concerns about whether the settlement was enough to deal with the impacts of the Sixties Scoop. Their mission is to promote reconciliation, healing and education. They also advocate for Survivors and their families.

Gathering of Survivors

In 2017, the Legacy of Hope Foundation, with the Sixties Scoop Healing Network, invited a group of Survivors from across Canada to meet for several days. They gave testimonials about their life experiences and trusted the LHF to be the stewards of their truths so that the LHF could develop an exhibit called "Bi-Giwen: Truth-Telling from the Sixties Scoop." This exhibit would forever capture their history and educate Canadians about this dark chapter. Nina Segalowitz (centre) is seen here with Tauni Sheldon and her son.

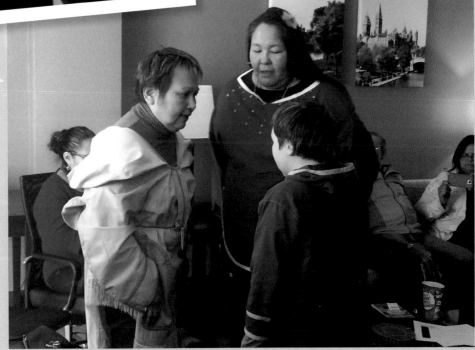

A gift blanket

Gift blankets are an important practice amongst some Indigenous Peoples. Items placed on the blanket are gifts for sharing. This gift blanket was created for the LHF's Bi-Giwen gathering. It celebrated the coming together of so many Sixties Scoop Survivors who bravely shared their stories as a part of their healing journeys.

Support and healing

For many, retelling such difficult experiences can be distressing, not only for the Survivors but also for their loved ones. The LHF worked hard to ensure a supportive and healing experience for this important work. This photo features Survivors, their loved ones and LHF staff as they gathered to share their stories for the Bi-Giwen project.

Creating awareness and understanding
Using Survivor stories, this travelling exhibit organized by the Sixties Scoop Indigenous Society of Alberta (SSISA), promoted greater understanding and empathy amongst Albertans about the Sixties Scoop and its impacts. Exhibits do important groundwork to raise awareness and build understanding amongst the public. They encourage empathy and understanding and inspire Canadians to support Survivors and to improve relationships with Indigenous Peoples.

Retelling such difficult experiences can be distressing, not only for the Survivors but also their loved ones.

Led by Survivors
Conrad Prince is the first director of engagement for the Sixties Scoop Healing Foundation. "Our mission is to accompany Survivors and their descendants along their healing journey by supporting cultural reclamation and reunification, holistic wellness services, advocacy, commemoration and educational initiatives." The Foundation has a Survivor-led volunteer board of directors working to fulfill its mission.

CHAPTER 5

The Modern System (1990–2023)

The Millennium Scoop

In 2021, Statistics Canada reported that 53.8 percent of children in care were Indigenous, and that many more Indigenous people lived in low-income households than non-Indigenous people. Indigenous families are also much more likely than non-Indigenous families to be struggling with poverty and overcrowded housing. Most Indigenous families are headed by a single mother. Many social workers use these situations to remove children from their homes and list poverty as the reason. The cause is both the colonial history and the ongoing systemic discrimination that have separated Indigenous Peoples from their families and relationships, land, medicine, language, practices, spirituality and traditions of well-being. In what is often referred to as the Millennium Scoop, thousands of Indigenous children continued to be apprehended during the 1990s and 2000s, and the rate of apprehension remains high.

Need for more foster homes
Dylan Cohen is pictured here speaking at a youth rally in Vancouver in 2018. Dylan and his twin sister were taken into care in their early teens when their mother, a Survivor of the Sixties Scoop herself, could no longer take care of them. Their first foster home was forty-five minutes away from their community in Winnipeg. "My social workers would always speak about the high caseloads and the limited number of foster homes . . . And for me that meant: 'we respect that this home isn't good for you, and that you're actually in a really bad place here, but it's probably the best' and that hurt a lot. That felt like I really just didn't matter more than the paycheque that I was to my foster parents, and the case file that I was for my agency." Dylan felt "like a cog in this giant machine . . . I know that with enough foster homes I could have stayed in my own community, and stayed in the same high school, instead of moving to three different schools, during some pretty formative years." Dylan went on to become an activist working for the First Call: BC Child and Youth Advocacy Coalition.

WATCH THE VIDEO

Watch the video at https://tinyurl.com/Calls-for-Change

Not defined by time in the system

Reina Foster, pictured here in 2018, is Anishinabek from Lac Seul First Nation, Ontario. She works in economic development for her community. Reina was two years old when she and her younger brother were first placed in care. Despite spending most of her childhood in care, she said she never lost hope. She was determined to protect her brother. Knowing that their home life had become unsafe, Reina made the difficult decision to ask for help. "I remember having a huge lump in my throat and all the memories from my childhood had rushed up, and I wasn't too sure what was going to happen to my brother and me. I wasn't too sure how we will be . . . processed I guess. I didn't know what was going to happen. But I knew that our safety and our protection mattered most. So I went through with the call."

WATCH THE VIDEO

Watch the video at http://tinyurl.com/Advocates-Call-for-Change

Police escort

Bridgitte Lopez was just four years old the first time she was apprehended and spent years in and out of foster care. She recalls how the social worker would show up at her house with the RCMP. The police cruiser would escort Bridgitte and the social worker away from the house until they got to the highway to make sure there was no trouble. Bridgitte points to the impacts of residential schools and the Sixties Scoop, saying "how many people my mom's age remember being young and taken away from their families and that's all that I remember . . . being young and being taken away from my family . . . As a kid I was thinking, 'I just want my mom.'" This is a picture of Bridgitte from September 2019.

Fighting for her family
Tamara Malcolm waged an eleven-year battle against the Manitoba child welfare system. She even went on social media to tell her story and gain support. She was eventually successful, and the family is focused on recovering. Tamara and her family are pictured here in November 2018.

WATCH THE VIDEO

Watch the video at
http://tinyurl.com/Tamara-Malcolm

"It's my firm belief that the foster care system is working the way it's designed: as a machine to destroy Indigeneity."

— Jaye Simpson

The system needs restructuring
Jaye Simpson, shown in this image from August 2020, was part of the Millennium Scoop. Jaye was removed from her mother and aunties when she was two years old. She spent years in foster care where she was sometimes abused. Many did not acknowledge her as Two Spirit. There are many challenges for Indigenous Two Spirit children in care.

"We need to look at how the system is removing Indigenous children from Indigenous mothers . . . An Indigenous mother may receive $600 on welfare to feed her children. The foster care system can say that's not good enough, take the child and put it in a home, and give that home $1800 to feed those children. So they're giving more money to non-Indigenous parents to feed Indigenous children, and they're not supplying Indigenous parents with any support."

— Jaye Simpson

Fighting Back

After the release of *No Quiet Place*, Indigenous Peoples continued to resist government child welfare practices. In response, in the 1990s the federal government began to transfer the administration of child and family services from the provinces and territories to Indigenous service providers. In 1998, Indigenous child and family service organizations from across Canada formed the First Nations Child and Family Caring Society "to support First Nations child and family service agencies in caring for First Nations children, youth and families."

Indigenous organizations and individuals continued to pressure the government for improvements in the child welfare system. At the same time, there were widespread demonstrations demanding more control over their land and their lives. The work continues. In 2023, the number of Indigenous children in the care of child welfare agencies remained unacceptably high and there were more children in care than there were in residential schools.

Community-led care
Indigenous communities have been fighting for control of their children's futures for decades.

FIRST NATIONS CHILD & FAMILY CARING SOCIETY OF CANADA

Working for equality

The First Nations Child and Family Caring Society of Canada (known as the Caring Society) was developed at a national meeting of First Nations child and family service agencies in Squamish First Nation, British Columbia, in 1998. The society works to ensure equal opportunities for First Nations children, youth and families to grow up safely at home, be healthy, get a good education and be proud of their culture. The Caring Society's logo is pictured here.

Protest march

This image shows a protest march at Allan Gardens, Toronto, in October 2011. Youth are protesting against the high apprehension of Indigenous children.

Idle No More

Idle No More is an ongoing protest movement, founded in December 2012 by four women: three First Nations women and one non-Indigenous ally. It is a grassroots movement among Indigenous Peoples in Canada. This image shows a January 2013 march towards the British Columbia Legislative Building. The Idle No More movement has raised awareness and brought a lot of attention to Indigenous issues across Canada. This is one way to put pressure on governments to live up to their commitments to Indigenous Peoples.

Youth in action

In 2013, this group of Cree youth walked 1,600 kilometres from their home in Whapmagoostui, Quebec, to Parliament Hill in Ottawa to bring attention to Indigenous issues. The walk began when David Kawapit Jr., seventeen, decided to trek to Ottawa to rally for better conditions for Canada's First Nations. After arriving, an exhausted Kawapit said the completed journey shows that youth can have a voice. Aboriginal Affairs Minister Bernard Valcourt acknowledged the determination and perseverance of the youths and committed to meet with the youths and offered to hear their concerns.

 **WATCH THE VIDEO**

Watch the video at
https://tinyurl.com/The-Journey-of-Nishiyuu

The Modern System (1990–2023)

A new way forward
These protesters are marching in May 2015 in support of Indigenous rights and equality for child welfare. In the centre front in black is Senator (then Chief Justice) Murray Sinclair, chair of the Truth and Reconciliation Commission.

Prayer walk
This image from December 2017 shows a prayer walk recognizing the fifth anniversary of the Idle No More movement. The participants' sign reads "Bring our Children Home." The event in Toronto, Ontario, illustrates the ongoing struggle to improve the child welfare system and the over-representation of Indigenous youth in care.

A group of Cree youth walked 1,600 kilometres from Whapmagoostui, Quebec, to Parliament Hill, Ottawa, to bring attention to Indigenous issues.

Canadian Human Rights Tribunal

Formed by Parliament in 1977, the Canadian Human Rights Tribunal (CHRT) is like a court of law, but it only hears cases relating to discrimination. In 2007, the Assembly of First Nations and the First Nations Child and Family Caring Society filed a complaint against the federal government, stating that 163,000 Indigenous children on reserve did not receive the same financial support that other Canadian children receive. In 2016, the CHRT agreed that the federal government was discriminating against Indigenous children in care on the reserve. Despite being ordered to stop its discriminatory practices, the federal government was slow to implement changes. It is vital that Canada recognizes and honours its commitment to the welfare of all children equally.

Filed a complaint of discrimination

In 2007, the Assembly of First Nations and the First Nations Child and Family Caring Society of Canada filed a complaint under the Canadian Human Rights Act. They alleged that Canada discriminates against First Nations children by consistently under-funding child welfare on reserves. Dr. Cindy Blackstock, executive director of the Caring Society, is a member of the Gitxsan First Nation. She is pictured here with Spirit Bear. In response to the complaint, the Department of Aboriginal Affairs put Blackstock under surveillance for "caring for First Nations children."

"I think that what is driving this is a colonial mindset," Blackstock said. "The federal government wants to call the shots and thinks Indigenous people should be grateful for what they are given. The problem with that is that these inequalities [in the child welfare system] have been known for more than 100 years."

Spirit Bear

Spirit Bear is a stuffed animal that represents the 163,000 First Nations children impacted by the First Nations child welfare case at the Canadian Human Rights Tribunal, as well as the thousands of other children who have committed to learning about the case and have taken part in peaceful and respectful actions in support of reconciliation and equity. Spirit Bear joined the Caring Society team in 2008 and was tasked with witnessing all of the tribunal hearings. In June 2017, Spirit Bear was awarded an honourary "Bearrister" degree from Osgoode Hall Law School. In October 2017, he was officially admitted to the "Bear" by the Indigenous Bar Association.

Ottawa discriminated against kids on reserves, human rights panel says

By The Canadian Press
⚠ Tue., Jan. 26, 2016 | ⏱ 4 min. read

Federal government charged with discrimination

In January 2016, the Canadian Human Rights Tribunal ruled that the federal government discriminated against First Nations children on racial grounds in its failure to provide the same level of welfare services that exist elsewhere. Dr. Cindy Blackstock said, "I can't think of a lower thing that a federal government can do than racially discriminate against . . . kids, know that they're doing it, know it is harming them by unnecessarily removing them from their families, have the recommendations in their hands where they could have made it better — and they don't do it."

Watch the video at
https://tinyurl.com/Ottawa-Seeks-Judicial-Review

Jordan's Principle

Dr. Cindy Blackstock, executive director of the First Nations Child and Family Caring Society, pictured here, fought for many years with the federal government over underfunding child welfare on reserves. In April 2016, the Canadian Human Rights Tribunal gave the Indigenous Affairs Department two weeks to confirm it has implemented Jordan's Principle. This is a policy designed to ensure First Nations children can access services without getting caught in red tape between federal/provincial/territorial funding responsibilities. The policy was named for a five-year-old Indigenous boy who died after a lengthy inter-government wrangle over who would pay for his home care.

Watch the video at
http://tinyurl.com/Canada-Fails-to-Comply

UPDATED DEC 24: NAN takes feds to Human Rights Tribunal over child welfare funding

A study found Tikinagan Child & Family Services requires 68 per cent more funding.

Dec 18, 2019 2:53 PM By: TbNewsWatch.com Staff

Non-compliance order

In December 2019, the Nishnawbe Aski Nation (NAN) took the federal government to the Canadian Human Rights Tribunal over the issue of funding for First Nations child welfare agencies. The Nation has asked for a non-compliance order against the government for its failure to change its funding formula to take into account the extra costs of providing services in remote communities.

"First Nations children actually receive far less government and public services than . . . other Canadians enjoy."

— Dr. Cindy Blackstock

CANADA

Canada accused of continued short-changing of First Nations kids, despite order to stop

By Anna McMillan · Global News
Posted February 5, 2021 2:04 pm

Problems persist

This February 2021 *Global News* article reported that Canada was accused of continued short-changing of First Nations kids, despite an order to stop. In 2021, the First Nations Child and Family Caring Society filed a non-compliance motion on the 2016 Canadian Human Rights Tribunal (CHRT) ruling that said families on reserve and in Yukon were being denied equitable child welfare services.

The Modern System (1990–2023)

Indigenous Children in Foster Care

■ **Percent of population that is Indigenous**

■ **Percent of children in foster care that are Indigenous**

The numbers in brackets show the date of the most recent statistics available.

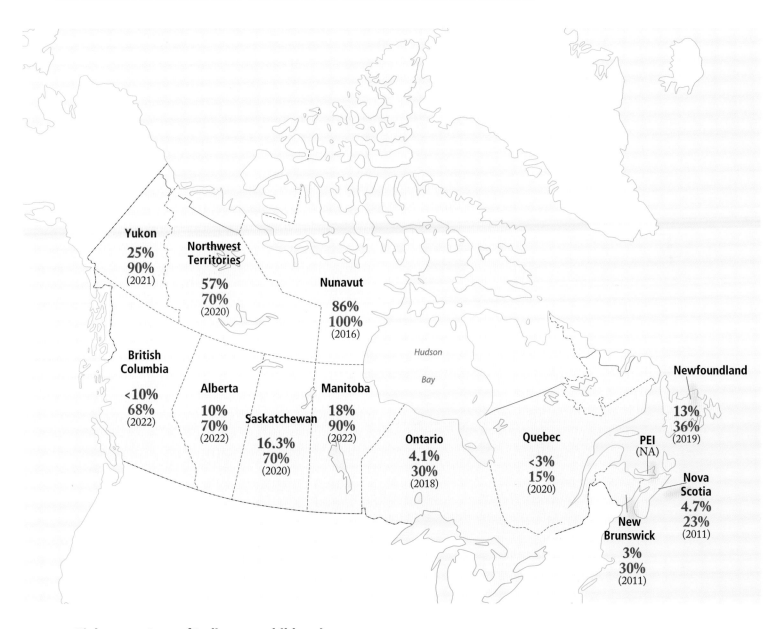

Yukon
25%
90%
(2021)

Northwest Territories
57%
70%
(2020)

Nunavut
86%
100%
(2016)

Hudson Bay

British Columbia
<10%
68%
(2022)

Alberta
10%
70%
(2022)

Saskatchewan
16.3%
70%
(2020)

Manitoba
18%
90%
(2022)

Ontario
4.1%
30%
(2018)

Quebec
<3%
15%
(2020)

Newfoundland
13%
36%
(2019)

PEI
(NA)

Nova Scotia
4.7%
23%
(2011)

New Brunswick
3%
30%
(2011)

High percentage of Indigenous children in care

Across Canada, Indigenous children comprise only 7.7 percent of the child population under fifteen years of age but make up 53.8 percent of the children in care. Changes are necessary to address the imbalance. In 2022, Dr. Cindy Blackstock stated, "Reconciliation means learning from past injustices in a way that changes behaviour and attitudes to prevent the injustices from continuing so that we can raise a generation of First Nations, Métis and Inuit children who do not have to recover from their childhoods and a generation of non-Indigenous children who never have to say they are sorry."

The Final Settlement Agreement

Following the Canadian Human Rights Tribunal ruling that the federal government discriminated against First Nations children, there was hope that the First Nations Child and Family Services Program would be fixed. But the government did nothing. After four years without improvements, the Assembly of First Nations took action. In 2020 they launched a class action lawsuit in court to force the federal government to provide compensation for the First Nations children and families who had been discriminated against dating back to 1991.

The First Nations Child and Family Caring Society of Canada (Caring Society) and Assembly of First Nations with others drafted a final settlement agreement for approval by the tribunal, and by the court. The settlement agreement outlined their terms: financial compensation and major changes to the way the Child and Family Services Program is run.

The long effort by the federal government to defeat these claims failed. On July 26, 2023, the Canadian Human Rights Tribunal approved the final settlement agreement, saying in part that "First Nations children ought to be honored for who they are, beautiful, valuable, strong and precious First Nations persons." The tribunal's approval also required the Minister of Indigenous Services to request an apology from the prime minister.

Continued activism
These First Nations singers were performing at a protest rally in Vancouver, British Columbia, on July 1, 2021. Their orange shirts reflect the history of residential schools as well as the systemic discrimination their peoples have faced under the Canadian government, including the Sixties Scoop and ongoing problems within the Child and Family Services Program. Continued activism and pressure finally pushed the government to sign the final settlement agreement.

Canadian Human Rights Tribunal
Tribunal canadien des droits de la personne
Ottawa, Canada K1A 1J4

July 26, 2023

By e-mail

(See Distribution List)

Dear Parties,

Re: First Nations Child and Family Caring Society et al. v. Attorney General of Canada
Tribunal File: T1340/7008

The Panel (Chair Marchildon and Member Lustig) wishes to provide the parties with the following decision with reasons to follow.

Ruling from the Bench akin to an oral ruling with reasons to follow on the Revised Agreement for compensation

Introduction

It took great leadership for the Assembly of First Nations (AFN) and Canada to collaborate and arrive at the previous historic Final Settlement Agreement (FSA). It took even greater leadership from the AFN and Canada's Ministers and their teams to receive the Tribunal's criticism of some aspects of the FSA (for example, leaving out some of the victims/survivors already recognized by this Tribunal), consult the Chiefs-in-Assembly, bring the Caring Society back to the negotiation table and arrive at this transformative and unprecedented Revised Settlement Agreement. According to the parties, this is the largest compensation settlement in Canadian history and it now includes a commitment from the Minister of Indigenous Services to request an apology from the Prime Minister. The Tribunal believes this was an example of grace under pressure and commends the parties to the Revised Agreement and everyone involved for this outstanding achievement that will provide some measure of justice to First Nations children and families who have unjustly suffered because of their race instead of being treated honorably and justly. First Nations children ought to be honored for who they are, beautiful, valuable, strong and precious First Nations persons. Governments, leaders and adults in any Nation have the sacred responsibility to honor, protect and value children and youth, not harm them. Complete justice will be achieved when systemic racial discrimination no longer exists. The compensation in this case is only one component. The Tribunal assisted meaningfully by the parties, has always focused on the need for

The final settlement agreement

This is the first page of the 2023 decision of the Canadian Human Rights Tribunal to approve the final settlement agreement. "Governments, leaders and adults in any Nation have the sacred responsibility to honor, protect and value children and youth, not harm them. Complete justice will be achieved when systemic racial discrimination no longer exists."

"This is a welcome step forward compensating affected First Nations and families for the discrimination they experienced. I thank the representative plaintiffs for their strength throughout these proceedings, as they are long overdue for an acknowledgement of the harms experienced."

— Joanna Bernard, Assembly of First Nations Interim National Chief"

Compensating First Nations peoples

On October 24, 2023, the Federal Court of Canada also approved the settlement agreement. Under the agreement, $23.34 billion was to be paid by the government to compensate more than 300,000 First Nations children and families who experienced discrimination. If distributed evenly, compensation would approximate the cost of a four-year university education per individual. But not all the money would go to individuals. Some would support organizations that work on behalf of those impacted by the discriminatory system.

This October 2023 government news release announces the Federal Court approval for the final settlement agreement. If the approval of the agreement is not appealed within the sixty-day appeal period, implementation could begin later in 2024. The Assembly of First Nations is not responsible for distributing compensation, which will be managed by the Deloitte Class Action Administrators. In some cases, class action members will not receive direct payments under the agreement. Instead, they will benefit from program initiatives run by organizations who receive funding from the agreement.

In addition, the government agreed that the First Nations Child and Family Services Program would be substantially reformed. An additional $19.07 billion would be used to ensure equality of funding and resources for First Nations children and families. Cultural and community-based programs would be supported, especially in remote communities. And First Nations youth who reach the age of majority and no longer qualify to be in foster care would be given support to help them prepare for their future. The implementation of these reforms was to be overseen by First Nations peoples.

Federal Court approves settlement agreement to compensate First Nations children and families

From: Indigenous Services Canada

News release

October 24, 2023 — Ottawa, Traditional Algonquin Territory, Ontario — Indigenous Services Canada

Today, the Federal Court of Canada approved the First Nations Child and Family Services, Jordan's Principle, Trout and Kith Class Settlement Agreement, with reasons to follow. The agreement was reached between the Assembly of First Nations (AFN), the Moushoom and Trout class actions plaintiffs and Canada, with the support of the First Nations Child and Family Caring Society.

This First Nations-led agreement includes a total of $23.34 billion to compensate First Nations children and families who were harmed by discriminatory underfunding of the First Nations Child and Family Services (FNCFS) program and those impacted by the federal government's narrow definition of Jordan's Principle.

This is a very important milestone in the process towards compensating First Nations children and families for the harms they suffered. This agreement could not have been reached without the hard work of the Parties and First Nations leadership, who never wavered in their dedication and determination that First Nations children and families receive compensation.

If the approval of the agreement is not appealed within the 60-day appeal period following the issuance of the Federal Court's order on the settlement, the process to implement the settlement through the court ordered third-party administrator could begin later in 2024.

The Hope for Wellness Help Line, which provides immediate, toll-free telephone and online-chat-based support and crisis intervention to all Indigenous Peoples in Canada, is always available. This service is available 24/7 in English and French, and upon request in Cree, Ojibway, and Inuktitut. Counsellors are available by phone at 1-855-242-3310 or by online chat at hopeforwellness.ca.

"The approval of the compensation settlement agreement was made possible by the tireless advocacy of First Nations leaders . . . No child or family should ever have to face the harms suffered by so many First Nations children and families . . . This is a significant step forward. More to do."

— Gary Anandasangaree, Minister of Crown-Indigenous Relations

Healing within the Community

The Government of Canada has done a lot of damage to Indigenous families, communities and nations through its discriminatory child welfare policies and practices. Many Survivors, Indigenous youth, community organizations and their allies who have been affected by these policies are working to heal and reconnect with their culture. Healing practices take many forms. They can include peer support groups, talking with Elders and other therapy providers and traditional activities such as smudging and participating in sweat lodges. Many Indigenous treatments involve supporting the whole family. Books and documentaries share Survivor experiences and help others learn of the trauma associated with the Sixties Scoop. These books and documentaries build empathy and understanding of what happened to generations of families and teach what it means to be an ally.

Watch the video at
https://tinyurl.com/Preserving-Culture

Apology ceremony
An Elder conducts a traditional ceremony to begin the Canadian government's March 8, 2019, apology to Inuit for forced tuberculosis relocations and the way the government mishandled the Inuit tuberculosis epidemic.

Reclaiming an Indigenous identity
Sarah Wright Cardinal is a Cree educator from northern Treaty 8 territory with Coast Salish, Dene and Nuu-chah-nulth extended family relations. Her work centres on the importance of healing from the colonial policies and practices that tried to assimilate Indigenous Peoples into non-Indigenous society. She is the author of *Beyond the Sixties Scoop: Reclaiming Indigenous Identity, Reconnection to Place, and Reframing Understandings of Being Indigenous.*

Trauma therapy helps healing

Angela Ashawasegai, pictured here, provides essential healing and support for Indigenous families and communities. Angela is a trained trauma therapist. She uses her skills, as well as her life experience as a Sixties Scoop Survivor, to help her clients overcome trauma and other mental health challenges.

Online Survivor support groups

For Indigenous Peoples, healing is often a group effort. Online Survivor groups, such as the Sixties Scoop Network, are vital parts of the healing work being done in communities across Canada. Survivors use social media to share experiences or raise awareness. Online communities can provide connection and support for Survivors on their healing journey, as well as create opportunities for in-person gatherings, like the one pictured here in March 2017.

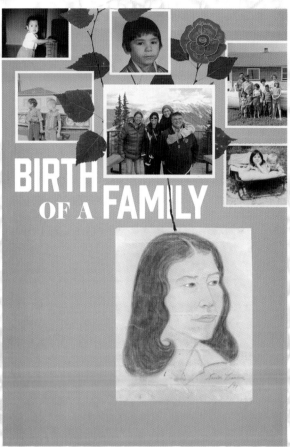

Sharing stories of survival

Personal stories and experiences help us understand the difficulties for individuals and families who were harmed in the Sixties Scoop. This movie poster is for an important documentary, *Birth of a Family*, directed by Tasha Hubbard in 2017. It tells the story of her four siblings who were taken from their Dene mother during the Sixties Scoop. The movie follows the family's journey to reunite after decades apart and heal together as a family.

Indigenous studies

Many universities and colleges have Indigenous studies programs. Scholars, both Indigenous and non-Indigenous, have been researching the effects of intergenerational trauma as well as the many different ways of healing and moving forward. This is an image of "Bi-Giwen: Truth-Telling from the Sixties Scoop." The exhibition was on display at the University of Ottawa on loan from the Legacy of Hope Foundation.

Reconnecting with Culture

Many studies have been done on how best to help Indigenous Peoples affected by colonial and oppressive policies and practices, such as the Sixties Scoop. Encouraging Indigenous reconnection with culture, and using cultural models of healing and well-being, have proven to be very effective. Indigenous and other governments are beginning to realize that funding to support cultural reclamation and on-the-land healing is important. These can support healing from the shame, guilt and poor feelings children once felt about being Indigenous because of their experiences with residential/day school and/or within the child welfare system.

Community events foster pride in traditions
Events like this one on the Musqueam First Nation reserve, British Columbia, are often organized by younger members of the community. They are a way to honour Elders and provide opportunities for people of all ages to learn about, and reconnect with, their cultural roots.

Indigenous Games
Ojibwe Anishinaabe Grandmother Kim Wheatley, known for her passion for Indigenous Knowledge, is seen here announcing the 2017 North American Indigenous Games. Kim brings Indigenous culture to sports and other events.

The land, nature and healing

For some Survivors, being out on the land can help foster healing by reconnecting with nature. Survivors can build confidence through learning traditional skills like hunting, gathering wild foods and medicines and taking part in ceremony. Returning to these traditional practices has restored cultural pride and community connections, which were previously negatively impacted.

WATCH THE VIDEO

Watch the video at
https://tinyurl.com/Reclaiming-His-Culture

Connecting to culture through dance

Indigenous Peoples have many types of social gatherings and dances that celebrate and honour their culture and history. This photo is taken from a Powwow, a cultural gathering that continues to be important for many Indigenous Peoples.

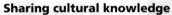

Sharing cultural knowledge

Former Legacy of Hope Foundation president, Richard Kistabish, is seen here speaking with children. Connecting youth with Canadian and Indigenous history in age-appropriate ways helps to educate Canadians about all the greatness of Indigenous Peoples. It also helps to address stereotypes, discriminatory beliefs that they may have learned from their parents. It contributes to creating better relationships between Indigenous and non-Indigenous people and a brighter future for generations to follow.

Reconnecting with Culture

Raising a monumental pole

Until 1951, monumental poles (formerly called totem poles), along with other Indigenous cultural practices, were banned. Poles were often burned or stolen and sent to museums. For many First Nations on the west coast of British Columbia, monumental poles document important stories and histories of the community. Raising a pole, pictured here, is a day-long event, bringing the whole community together for a shared purpose. Continuing this tradition shows resilience and cultural pride. Strengthening traditional and cultural roots often helps Survivors by providing a sense of connection to others and can significantly help with healing from past traumas.

Saving Indigenous languages

Language is a fundamental part of any culture. Most children of the Sixties Scoop who were adopted outside of their communities were not allowed to speak their language in their new home. That is why language revitalization is an essential part of healing and reconciliation for Indigenous communities. This sign in English and Inuktitut is an example of the Indigenous language renewal that is taking place across the country.

Passing down cultural traditions

Many Indigenous parents are reconnecting with their traditional language and culture and passing them on to their children. This Inuit mother from Nunavut is wearing a traditional style amouti, a special parka with a large hood for carrying her child. It is a great way for a mother to keep her child warm and close while she goes about her day.

Healing through traditional arts

The Aboriginal Healing Foundation did research on healing through the creative arts and found that "activities like beading, sewing, knitting, and carving are, in the end, spoken about . . . as being therapeutic. They find it grounding, centring, a way of being at peace within themselves."

This image shows purple beaded hearts that were made during a healing activity.

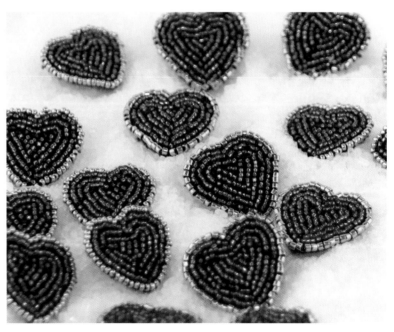

Reconnecting with Culture   99

The Work of Reconciliation

There have been many lawsuits and efforts by Indigenous Peoples to hold the Government of Canada accountable for its unjust child welfare practices. As a result of this resistance, the government has enacted new legislation to reduce the number of Indigenous children and youth in care and improve child and family services. An Act Respecting First Nations, Inuit and Métis Children, Youth and Families came into effect on January 1, 2020. The Assembly of First Nations and the Canadian government worked together to determine how the Act would be implemented. The Act affirms the rights of First Nations, Inuit and Métis Peoples to exercise jurisdiction over child and family services in their own communities. It is important to recognize that Indigenous Peoples always had this right, but through this law, Canada now recognizes that right. It will take many years to right the wrongs of the Sixties Scoop and establish new relationships between Indigenous Peoples and Canada. Much of this fight for change has fallen on the shoulders of Indigenous Peoples. Canadians must face truths about the harms done through the child welfare system and take part in supporting solutions and being allies. This is an essential step on the path to reconciliation.

Support for the whole family
Entire Indigenous communities were the targets of colonial policies. Community-based healing starts with a reclamation of Indigenous culture and tradition, and greater recognition of the inherent right of Indigenous Peoples to decide what is best for their children. Many Indigenous communities offer parenting classes and better support to families in need to directly address the impacts of the Sixties Scoop.

Bring our children home

Artist, storyteller and father of four, Bomgiizhik (Isaac Murdoch) is from Nimkii Aazhibikoong First Nation, Ontario. His artwork often references the issues that face Indigenous Peoples. This painting, *Children Home Tipi*, depicts his dream for children removed from their homes to be able to return to their communities, embrace their culture and heal. "One nation cannot take another nation's children. That's genocide. Let's do all we can to bring our children home."

A new way forward

This is the title page of An Act Respecting First Nations, Inuit and Métis Children, Youth and Families that came into effect on January 1, 2020. Under the Act, Indigenous Nations can make a coordination agreement with the Canadian government. Once in place, the nation can establish Indigenous laws regarding their child and family services that prevail over all other conflicting federal, provincial and territorial laws. It "gives them the ability to decide what is best for their children, their families and communities."

CANADA

CONSOLIDATION

CODIFICATION

An Act respecting First Nations, Inuit and Métis children, youth and families

Loi concernant les enfants, les jeunes et les familles des Premières Nations, des Inuits et des Métis

S.C. 2019, c. 24

L.C. 2019, ch. 24

Current to April 4, 2023

Last amended on January 1, 2020

À jour au 4 avril 2023

Dernière modification le 1 janvier 2020

Published by the Minister of Justice at the following address:
http://laws-lois.justice.gc.ca

Publié par le ministre de la Justice à l'adresse suivante :
http://lois-laws.justice.gc.ca

New child welfare agreement

Pictured here in July 2021, Cowessess First Nation and Prime Minister Justin Trudeau signed the Cowessess First Nation Miyo Pimatisowin Act. It details how this nation reclaims oversight of child welfare through its own agency and control. "Today is an example of how reconciliation is possible in Canada . . . with Cowessess First Nation in the driver's seat . . . we stand ready to enter a new chapter of our history that will bring new support, hope, and opportunity to Cowessess First Nation children and youth." — Cadmus Delorme, Chief, Cowessess First Nation

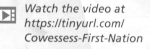

Watch the video at
https://tinyurl.com/
Cowessess-First-Nation

The Cowessess First Nation approach to child welfare

Mia Buckles from the Cowessess First Nation Youth Council is seen here speaking at the signing ceremony. Cowessess First Nation's approach to child welfare is very different from the provincial approach. "In Saskatchewan, 86 per cent of children in care are First Nations, and 150 of them are from Cowessess . . . It's their time to receive the opportunity to come home and heal with their families, on their own land through a holistic approach . . . After years of our children being taken and separated from their families, culture and, ultimately, their senses of themselves, we are one step closer to breaking one of the many generational curses that bind us."

Celebrating the new law

Dancers perform for Prime Minister Justin Trudeau, Cowessess First Nation Chief Cadmus Delorme and the community. While there was much to celebrate, there was still more work to be done. As of October 31, 2022, twenty-two other First Nations across Canada were in the process of coordinating child welfare agreements with the government.

Peguis First Nation takes control of community child welfare

In January 2022, the Peguis First Nation, Manitoba, signed a historic child welfare agreement with the federal government. It gives the community authority over how child welfare is administered.

Wabaseemoong First Nation signs new child welfare agreement

In August 2021, the Wabaseemoong First Nation, Ontario, signed an agreement with the federal government. The new child welfare legislation means Indigenous Peoples are better able to protect their children from being removed from their communities.

Timeline

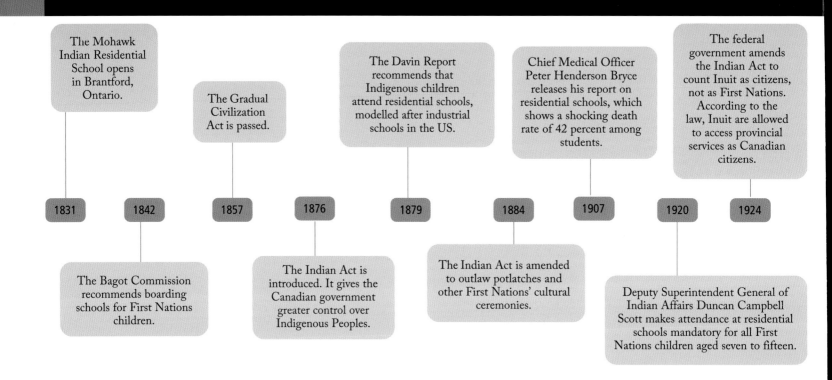

The Mohawk Indian Residential School opens in Brantford, Ontario.

The Gradual Civilization Act is passed.

The Davin Report recommends that Indigenous children attend residential schools, modelled after industrial schools in the US.

Chief Medical Officer Peter Henderson Bryce releases his report on residential schools, which shows a shocking death rate of 42 percent among students.

The federal government amends the Indian Act to count Inuit as citizens, not as First Nations. According to the law, Inuit are allowed to access provincial services as Canadian citizens.

1831 1842 1857 1876 1879 1884 1907 1920 1924

The Bagot Commission recommends boarding schools for First Nations children.

The Indian Act is introduced. It gives the Canadian government greater control over Indigenous Peoples.

The Indian Act is amended to outlaw potlatches and other First Nations' cultural ceremonies.

Deputy Superintendent General of Indian Affairs Duncan Campbell Scott makes attendance at residential schools mandatory for all First Nations children aged seven to fifteen.

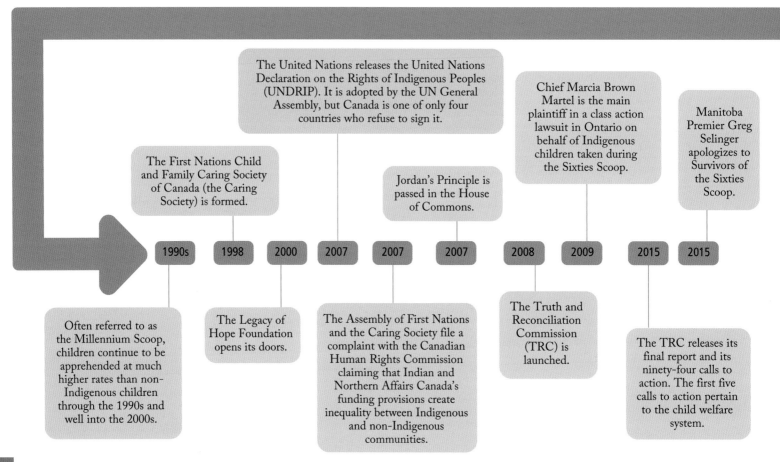

The United Nations releases the United Nations Declaration on the Rights of Indigenous Peoples (UNDRIP). It is adopted by the UN General Assembly, but Canada is one of only four countries who refuse to sign it.

Chief Marcia Brown Martel is the main plaintiff in a class action lawsuit in Ontario on behalf of Indigenous children taken during the Sixties Scoop.

Manitoba Premier Greg Selinger apologizes to Survivors of the Sixties Scoop.

The First Nations Child and Family Caring Society of Canada (the Caring Society) is formed.

Jordan's Principle is passed in the House of Commons.

1990s 1998 2000 2007 2007 2007 2008 2009 2015 2015

Often referred to as the Millennium Scoop, children continue to be apprehended at much higher rates than non-Indigenous children through the 1990s and well into the 2000s.

The Legacy of Hope Foundation opens its doors.

The Assembly of First Nations and the Caring Society file a complaint with the Canadian Human Rights Commission claiming that Indian and Northern Affairs Canada's funding provisions create inequality between Indigenous and non-Indigenous communities.

The Truth and Reconciliation Commission (TRC) is launched.

The TRC releases its final report and its ninety-four calls to action. The first five calls to action pertain to the child welfare system.

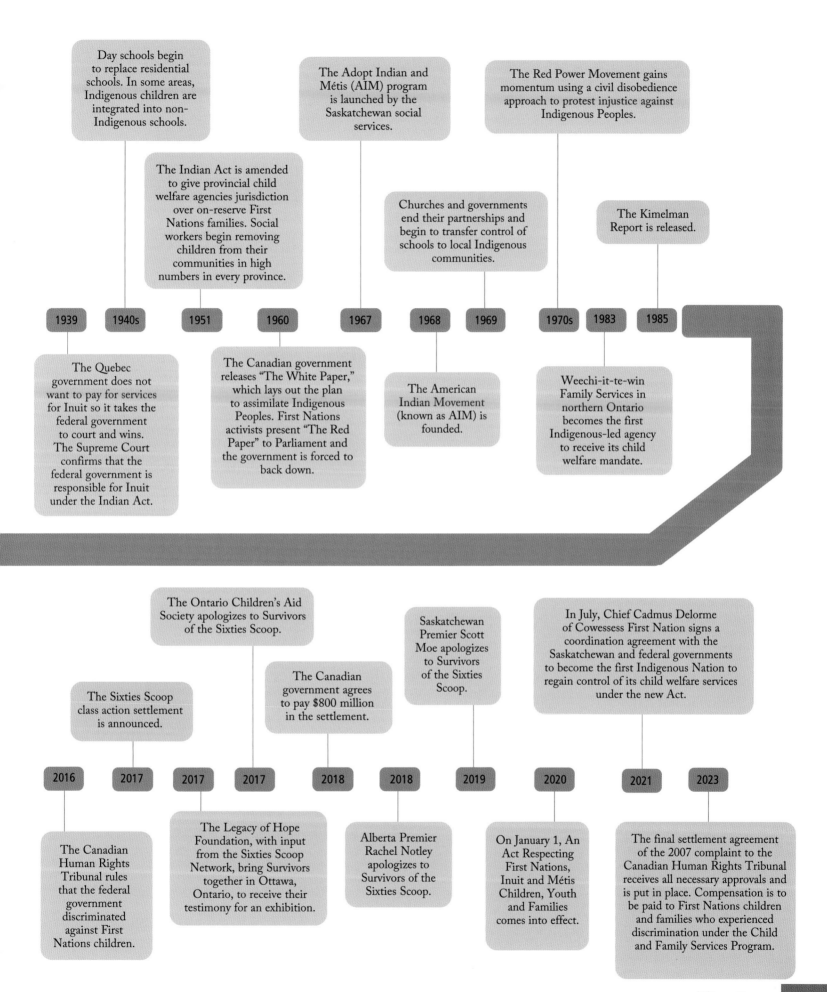

1939
The Quebec government does not want to pay for services for Inuit so it takes the federal government to court and wins. The Supreme Court confirms that the federal government is responsible for Inuit under the Indian Act.

Day schools begin to replace residential schools. In some areas, Indigenous children are integrated into non-Indigenous schools.

1940s

The Indian Act is amended to give provincial child welfare agencies jurisdiction over on-reserve First Nations families. Social workers begin removing children from their communities in high numbers in every province.

1951

1960
The Canadian government releases "The White Paper," which lays out the plan to assimilate Indigenous Peoples. First Nations activists present "The Red Paper" to Parliament and the government is forced to back down.

The Adopt Indian and Métis (AIM) program is launched by the Saskatchewan social services.

1967

1968
The American Indian Movement (known as AIM) is founded.

Churches and governments end their partnerships and begin to transfer control of schools to local Indigenous communities.

1969

The Red Power Movement gains momentum using a civil disobedience approach to protest injustice against Indigenous Peoples.

1970s
Weechi-it-te-win Family Services in northern Ontario becomes the first Indigenous-led agency to receive its child welfare mandate.

1983

The Kimelman Report is released.

1985

2016
The Canadian Human Rights Tribunal rules that the federal government discriminated against First Nations children.

2017
The Sixties Scoop class action settlement is announced.

2017
The Legacy of Hope Foundation, with input from the Sixties Scoop Network, bring Survivors together in Ottawa, Ontario, to receive their testimony for an exhibition.

The Ontario Children's Aid Society apologizes to Survivors of the Sixties Scoop.

2017

2018
The Canadian government agrees to pay $800 million in the settlement.

2018
Alberta Premier Rachel Notley apologizes to Survivors of the Sixties Scoop.

Saskatchewan Premier Scott Moe apologizes to Survivors of the Sixties Scoop.

2019

2020
On January 1, An Act Respecting First Nations, Inuit and Métis Children, Youth and Families comes into effect.

In July, Chief Cadmus Delorme of Cowessess First Nation signs a coordination agreement with the Saskatchewan and federal governments to become the first Indigenous Nation to regain control of its child welfare services under the new Act.

2021

2023
The final settlement agreement of the 2007 complaint to the Canadian Human Rights Tribunal receives all necessary approvals and is put in place. Compensation is to be paid to First Nations children and families who experienced discrimination under the Child and Family Services Program.

Glossary

Aboriginal: An older term used to describe First Nations, Inuit and later Métis as the original inhabitants of this land, now more commonly referred to as Indigenous.

Adopt Indian and Métis (AIM): Saskatchewan's targeted Indigenous transracial adoption program.

Aging out: When children in care reach the age of majority (usually eighteen) in their jurisdiction, they are no longer eligible for provincial government support and must "age out" of the child welfare system.

American Indian Movement (AIM): An Indigenous grassroots movement founded in Minneapolis, Minnesota, in July 1968 to address systemic issues of poverty, discrimination and police brutality against First Nations living in the US.

Assimilation: When the culture of a minority or immigrant group becomes lost within another, more dominant, culture.

Bias: A preference or tendency to think or act in a certain way. It could be positive or negative.

Canadian Human Rights Act: The Canadian Human Rights Act is a statute passed by the Parliament of Canada in 1977. It states that all Canadians have the right to equality, equal opportunity, fair treatment and an environment free of discrimination.

Canadian Human Rights Tribunal: Created by Parliament in 1977, the Canadian Human Rights Tribunal decides whether a person or organization has engaged in a discriminatory practice as defined under the Canadian Human Rights Act.

Child welfare system: A set of government and private services licensed and overseen by the provincial government and intended to protect children from abuse and neglect and encourage family stability.

Civil rights: The basic rights and privileges that come with being a member of society in a country. These can include things such as the right to vote, to have an education and to receive justice in the courts.

Class action lawsuit: A type of lawsuit where one of the parties is a group of people who are represented collectively by a member or members of that group.

Colonialism: The policy or practice of acquiring full or partial political control over another country, occupying it with settlers and exploiting it economically.

Compensation: The payment of money to make up for a wrong that was done to a person or group.

Cultural identity: This is the shared characteristics of a group of people, which encompasses place of birth, religion, language, cuisine, social behaviours, values, art, literature and music. Every culture can teach us about ourselves, others and the global community.

Culturally-appropriate care: Refers to care and services that are sensitive to people's cultural identity or heritage.

Cultural genocide: Destroying anything that identifies a group of people as distinct, such as language, tradition and values.

Culture: The customs, traditions and values of a nation or its people.

Day school: Day school students remained in their communities and went home to their families in the evenings. They gradually replaced residential schools but were run by the same teachers, priests, nuns and administrators until the late 1990s.

Delegation: A small group of people who are generally appointed to represent a much larger group's ideas or demands.

Discrimination: Unjust actions that are caused by a particular mindset or prejudice. A means of treating people negatively because of their group identity. Discrimination may be based on nationhood, language, age, ancestry, gender, sexual orientation, culture, religion or spiritual beliefs and ceremonies, political beliefs, physical or mental disability, appearance or economic and family status. Acts of discrimination hurt, humiliate and isolate the victim.

Enfranchisement: A legal process for terminating a person's Indian status under the Indian Act. This was also a means of enacting government discipline, punishing and silencing Indigenous Peoples who were vocal in their opposition of government policies. Removing status was the ultimate way for the government to carry out threats against Indigenous Peoples and inhibit political opposition.

First Nations: Original nations in Canada who are neither Inuit nor Métis. There are over 600 First Nations communities and over 50 nations and languages in Canada.

Heritage: Traditions passed down to younger generations.

Immigration: The arrival of people into a country from their homeland.

Indian: A term formerly used to describe Indigenous Peoples in Canada and the US. Like "Eskimo," this term has mostly fallen out of use.

Indigenous: Refers to people who originate in a place or are native to a place or country. Similar to Aboriginal, it includes First Nations, Inuit and Métis.

Indigenous Peoples: Refers to the original nations of this land — First Nations — and now also includes Inuit and Métis. The "s" on Peoples is intentional to demonstrate there are more than fifty nations included in First Nations alone, many with different languages, cultures, diets, traditions, ceremonies, etc.

Industrial school: Established on and off reservations to train Indigenous children in trades and to assimilate them into white society. Schools typically had a half-day policy where students were expected to attend class for half a day and work during the other half. These schools were government-owned and church-run.

Injustice: A wrongful action taken against an individual or group that denies them their basic rights.

Integration: Combining one group into another, such as a racial, ethnic or religious group.

Inuit: Original Peoples who mainly reside in the Canadian Arctic. Inuit were formerly referred to as "Eskimo."

Kinship ties: The culturally defined relationships between individuals. All kinship ties are based on family and community connections. Kinship is a basis for forming social groups and for classifying people. There is a great variety in kinship rules and patterns across Indigenous communities.

Language revitalization: A movement to halt or reverse the decline of traditional languages or to revive a language at risk of becoming extinct.

Millennium Scoop: The Millennium Scoop was coined to describe the alarming rate at which child welfare agencies in Canada continue to take Indigenous children into out-of-home care. It began in the early 1980s. As of 2023, there were more Indigenous children in the care of the child welfare system than there were in residential schools.

Métis: The Métis are historically descendants of First Nations–European unions.

Native: Being the first people to populate an area. Native people in what is now Canada are First Nations and Inuit.

Non-compliance order: Failure to obey a law or failure to comply with the law.

Oppression: The legal rights, freedoms, culture, languages, ideas or demands of an individual or group of people are not recognized, allowed to be expressed or are criminalized by authorities such as the government, justice system, police or military.

Overrepresentation: Defined as the appearance of a group in a category that exceeds expectations for that group or differs substantially from the representation of others in that category. For example, more Indigenous children are in care than would be expected by their population numbers compared to non-Indigenous children; Indigenous children are overrepresented in the child welfare system.

Plaintiff: A person who brings a case against another person or organization in a court of law.

Potlatch: Meaning "to give" in Chinook. Potlatch is an event that celebrates social changes such as births, deaths, marriages and the appointment of a new chief.

Powwow: A Powwow is a ceremony that involves praying while dancing, singing or drumming. Powwows can celebrate different occasions and thank Mother Earth for all that she has provided. Today there are traditional and competitive Powwows.

Prejudice: An attitude, usually negative, directed toward a person or group of people based on wrong or distorted information. Prejudiced thinking may result in acts of discrimination.

Propaganda: The spread of specific information, ideas or images to control public opinion or actions. An example is the residential school video created in the 1950s that showed seemingly happy Indigenous children at school and put forth the idea that it was in the best interest of the children to attend residential school. Video link: http://tinyurl.com/rcwresidential066

Race: The idea that people can be divided into different groups based on physical characteristics that they are perceived to share such as skin colour or eye shape. Race is defined by society and is not an actual biological difference between people.

Racism: A belief that one nation is superior to another. People are not treated as equals because of their cultural or ethnic differences. Racism may be systemic (part of institutions, governments, organizations and programs) or part of the attitudes and behaviours of individuals.

Redress: To right a wrong, sometimes by compensating the victim or by punishing the wrongdoer. Refers to the movement within the Indigenous community seeking an official apology and redress for the injustices related to the residential school system and the Sixties Scoop.

Reserve: Indian reserves were areas of property set aside by the Crown for First Nations Peoples. Under the Indian Act, the Minister of Indian Affairs was given jurisdiction over reserves.

Residential schools: These were boarding schools that were government-owned and church-run. Indigenous children were taken from their homes and families and sent to residential schools, often against their will.

Royal Canadian Mounted Police (RCMP): Also known as the Mounties, these law enforcement officers are known for their red coats and patrolling on horseback. They played key roles in the removal of children from their homes along with the child welfare system.

Segregation: The policy or practice of separating people of different races, classes or ethnic groups, especially as a form of discrimination.

Sixties Scoop: The large-scale removal or "scooping" of Indigenous children by provincial government social service agencies. Children were removed from their homes, communities and families beginning in the 1960s and placed into predominantly non-Indigenous, middle-class families across Canada and internationally.

Sweat lodge: Ceremonial sweat bath used in purification rituals. Sweat lodges are made of natural substances, such as animal skins, stone and wood.

The Red Power Movement: The phrase "Red Power" is attributed to author Vine Deloria, Jr. It commonly expressed a growing sense of pan-Indian identity in the late 1960s among First Nations in the United States.

Treaty: An agreement made between two or more sovereign parties. Indigenous Peoples signed treaties amongst themselves prior to contact. After settlers arrived, treaties were made between Indigenous Peoples and colonial governments. The Supreme Court of Canada has ruled that treaties must be interpreted by both what was written (which did not always reflect what was discussed or agreed to) and the oral traditions of the Indigenous parties to the treaties.

Truth and Reconciliation Commission (TRC): The TRC was created to investigate and discover the truth about the treatment of students at residential schools and to facilitate reconciliation.

Tuberculosis (TB): An infection of the lungs that is contagious and may cause death.

UNDRIP: On June 21, 2021, the United Nations Declaration on the Rights of Indigenous Peoples Act received Royal Assent in Canada and came into force. It is about the respect, recognition and protection of the human rights of Indigenous Peoples.

Visible minority: This is a modern term used to describe people of an ethnic group who have physical features, usually skin colour, that make them distinct from the majority of the population.

Youth in care: Children who have been removed from their original family by child welfare services because authorities have deemed their family unable or unfit to look after them properly. In Canada, the majority of Indigenous children are removed from their families due to poverty.

For Further Reading and Additional Resources

For Further Reading

Chapter 1
As Long as the Rivers Flow. Larry Loyie with Constance Brissenden; illustrations by Heather D. Holmlund. Groundwood Books 2002. Larry Loyie is ten and about to be sent to his first year of residential school, but before he has to go his family spends the summer teaching him the lessons and wisdom they hold dear. This book reinforces the traditional roles Elders played in teaching Indigenous children before colonization.

Chapter 2
Muinji'j Asks Why: The Story of the Mi'kmaq and the Shubenacadie Residential School. Shanika MacEachern, Breighlynn MacEachern; illustrations by Zeta Paul. Nimbus 2022. A young Mi'kmaw girl is told about the residential school her family and people were forced to attend and the ways in which the government made decisions for her people, not with them.

No Time to Say Goodbye: Children's Stories of Kuper Island Residential School. Sylvia Olsen; with Rita Morris and Ann Sam. Sononis 2003. Five children from a Saanich village in British Columbia are suddenly taken to a residential school on an isolated island. A fictional account based on recollections of Tsartlip First Nation members who survived the Kuper Island residential school.

Shin-chi's Canoe. Nicola I. Campbell; pictures by Kim LaFave. Groundwood Books 2008. In the sequel to *Shi-shi-etko*, Shi-shi-etko tries to help her little brother during his last days at home before Shin-chi starts residential school himself. *Shin-chi's Canoe* speaks to the experiences of children in residential school and the loss of culture and family they experienced.

The 500 Years of Resistance Comic Book. Gord Hill. Arsenal Pulp Press 2010. This graphic book chronicles Indigenous resistance and protests across North and South America from Christopher Columbus to 2006. The book discusses residential schools and their direct ties to assimilationist policies.

Chapter 3
Ohpikiihaakan-ohpihmeh Raised Somewhere Else: A 60s Scoop Adoptee's Story of Coming Home. Colleen Cardinal. Roseway 2018. Colleen Cardinal's personal memoir tells her story of being an Indigenous child who grew up in a non-Indigenous household as a Sixties Scoop adoptee.

These are the Stories. Christine Miskonoodinkwe. Kegedonce Press 2021. Presented in short chapters and comprising the life of Sixties Scoop Survivor Christine Miskonoodinkwe Smith, this memoir reveals the author's experiences in the child welfare system and her journey towards healing.

Chapter 5
A Girl Called Echo. Katherena Vermette; illustrated by Scott B. Henderson, Donovan Yaciuk. Highwater Press 2017. Echo Desjardins is a thirteen-year-old Métis girl who feels lost and alone in a new school. This series follows a young girl living in a foster home as she discovers a culture and identity she has been disconnected from.

Chapter 6
Indigenous Peoples Atlas of Canada. The Royal Canadian Geographical Society/Canadian Geographic. Kids Can Press 2018. Inspired by the Truth and Reconciliation Commission's calls to action, this book shares the experiences, perspectives and histories of First Nations, Inuit and Métis Peoples. The themes explored range from language and culture to history, treaties and residential schools.

21 Things You May Not Know about the Indian Act: Helping Canadians Make Reconciliation with Indigenous Peoples a Reality. Bob Joseph. Indigenous Relations Press 2018. Bob Joseph's guide to understanding the dated legal jargon of the Indian Act while examining ways Indigenous Peoples can break free of its archaic grip highlights how reading the Indian Act is the key to making progress towards true reconciliation.

Legacy of Hope Foundation
Resources on the Sixties Scoop and child welfare system, including curricula, exhibitions, podcasts and other resources.

Additional Resources for Youth in Care

National Resources
C.A.R.E. Jeunesse (bilingual)
Website: https://en.carejeunesse.org/
Email: direction@carejeunesse.org
Phone: 514-307-2474

First Nations Child and Family Caring Society
Website: https://fncaringsociety.com/

Native Women's Association of Canada
Website: https://nwac.ca/programs

The National Youth in Care Network
Website: https://youthincare.ca/

Métis Nation Child and Family Services
Website: https://www.metisnation.ca/what-we-do/cfs

National Inuit Youth Council
Website: https://www.itk.ca/projects/national-inuit-youth-council/

Warrior Kids Podcast
Website: https://warriorkidspodcast.com/

Provincial Resources
Federation of BC Youth in Care Networks
Toll-Free: 1-800-565-8055
Website: www.fbcyicn.ca
Email: info@fbcyicn.ca

Partners For Youth Inc.
Fredericton, NB
Website: www.partnersforyouth.ca

Saskatchewan Youth in Care and Custody Network Inc.
Toll Free Youth Line: 1-888-528-8061
Website: www.syiccn.ca
Email: info@syiccn.ca

Voices: Manitoba's Youth in Care Network
Phone: 204-982-4956
Website: www.voices.mb.ca
Email: info@voices.mb.ca

YouthCAN (Ontario Youth Communication Advocacy Network)
Phone: 416-987-7725
Website: www.ontarioyouthcan.org

Yukon Child and Youth Advocate
Website: https://www.ycao.ca/

Visual Credits

Every effort has been made to locate the original copyright owners. If the reader has any additional information on the original copyright owners, we would be happy to include it in any revised editions.

DIAND – Department of Indian Affairs and Northern Development
LAC – Library and Archives Canada
LOHF – Legacy of Hope Foundation
NFBC – National Film Board of Canada

p. 6 (top, 1933-257-1) LAC. NFBC. William MacDougall.
p. 6 (bottom, e010864168) Department of Indian and Northern Affairs Canada.
p. 7 (top, 1970-188-2217; middle, 2838150) LAC.
p. 7 (bottom, R9266-3459) LAC. NFBC. Peter Winkworth.
p. 8 (top, e011156727) LAC. NFBC. Robert Bell.
p. 8 (bottom, NA-949-118) Glenbow Museum and Archives.
p. 9 (top, 1980-026-004) Canadian Museum of History. Jake Thomas Learning Centre.
p. 9 (bottom, 1973-84-1) LAC.
p. 10 (top, PA-059589) LAC. Duncan Campbell Scott.
p. 10 (bottom left, a102692-v6) LAC. DIAND. J. C. Jackson.
p. 11 (bottom, a100983-v8) LAC. DIAND.
p. 11 (top, PA-182269) LAC.
p. 12 (2485) Nova Scotia Archives. Micmac Camp.
p. 13 (bottom, PA-030779) LAC. John A. Brown.
p. 13 (top, NA-3941-5) Glenbow Museum and Archives.
p. 14 (top, P93-V-16) Provincial Archives of New Brunswick.
p. 14 (bottom, a166825) LAC. Richard Harrington.
p. 15 (top, e002265666) LAC. NFBC. Gar Lunney.
p. 15 (bottom, PA-189121) LAC. NFBC. Douglas Wilkinson.
p. 16 (top) University of Saskatchewan University Archives and Special Collections.
p. 16 (bottom, e011307232) LAC. DIAND. *Calgary Herald*.
p. 17 (top) University of Saskatchewan University Archives and Special Collections.
p. 17 (bottom left, PA-881-21) Glenbow Museum and Archives.
p. 17 (bottom right, e010948786) LAC. NFBC.
p. 18 (top, e004413803) LAC. James Vinton Stowell.
p. 18 (middle, a099430-v6) LAC. DIAND. Lachlan T. Burwash.
p. 18 (bottom, C-007819) LAC. John Woodruff.
p. 19 (middle, e011369233-017_s3; bottom, e011369233-018_s1). LAC. F. W. Waugh.
p. 20 (top, e011369233-023_s1) LAC. F. W. Waugh.
p. 20 (bottom, PA-060706) LAC. John Boyd.
p. 21 (top) Algoma University Shingwauk Residential Schools Centre.
p. 21 (bottom, e011306801) LAC. DIAND.
p. 22 (top right) The Indian Act. The Indian Residential School History and Dialogue Centre.
p. 22 (bottom left, e000009998) DIAND.
p. 23 (top, 1996-63) LAC. DIAND.
p. 23 (middle) Northern BC Archives. W. H. Collison.
p. 23 (bottom, LH-6235) Saskatoon Public Library.
p. 24 (top, LH-4072) Saskatoon Public Library.
p. 24 (middle left) The Indian Act. The Indian Residential School History and Dialogue Centre.
p. 24 (middle right, S-B-4698) Provincial Archives of Saskatchewan.
p. 24 (bottom) Hudson's Bay Company Archives. Richard Harrington.
p. 25 (top, LH-4071; middle right, PH-93-114-2) Saskatoon Public Library.
p. 25 (middle left, PAS, S-E19, File 36, Pass 68) Provincial Archives of Saskatchewan.
p. 25 (bottom, a110862-v6) LAC. S. J. Bailey.
p. 26 Kent Monkman. *The Scream*, 2017.
p. 27 (top right, C-003187) LAC.
p. 27 (top left, 29211) LAC. Indian Affairs Annual Reports, 1864 to 1990.
p. 27 (top, P75-103) Anglican Church of Canada. The General Synod Archives.
p. 27 (middle) Notre-Dame-du-Cap.
p. 27 (bottom) LAC. H. J. Woodside.
p. 28 (top, e01131146) LAC. DIAND.
p. 28 (middle, a100529-v6) LAC. DIAND. Oswald S. Finnie.

p. 28 (bottom, PA-048574) NFBC.
p. 29 (top, PA-182266) LAC.
p. 29 (bottom, e011165567) LAC. DIAND.
p. 30 (top, e011271701) LAC. Anne and Ryan Swain.
p. 30 (middle, PA-146509) LAC. NFBC. Douglas Wilkinson.
p. 30 (bottom, a101066-v6) LAC. DIAND. J. V. Jacobson.
p. 31 (top left, PA-042966) LAC. Topley Studio.
p. 31 (top right) P. H. Bryce, 1922.
p. 31 (bottom, e011080328_s) LAC. DIAND.
p. 32 (left) *The Summerland Review*, 1927.
p. 32 (right, e011078116) LAC. DIAND.
p. 33 (bottom, P75-103-S4-507; top, P75-103-S1-79) Anglican Church of Canada. The General Synod Archives.
p. 33 (middle) Aboriginal Healing Foundation. The Healing Has Begun.
p. 34 (top, PA-045174) LAC. Geological Survey of Canada.
p. 34 (bottom, PA-044539) LAC. Department of Interior Canada.
p. 35 (top, R-A2690) Provincial Archives of Saskatchewan.
p. 35 (bottom, PA-189088) LAC. NFBC.
p. 36 (left) Isaac Murdoch. *The Ones Who Stayed*, 2018.
p. 36 (right, C-10461) LAC.
p. 37 (top right, PA-16145) Bud Glunz. NFBC.
p. 37 (bottom left, e011308192) LAC. DIAND.
p. 37 (bottom right, e011307122) LAC. Jack Ablett.
p. 38 (top, e011307123) LAC. Jack Ablett.
p. 38 (middle, e002414899) LAC. Department of Health.
p. 38 (bottom, M2006-08 P078) Anglican Church of Canada. The General Synod Archives.
p. 39 (top) Rhonda Chapman.
p. 39 (middle right) *Winnipeg Free Press*, 1960.
p. 39 (bottom) LAC. George Mully.
p. 40 (top left, 19.3-1992-14-263) Mennonite Archives of Ontario.
p. 40 (top right, e011308323) LAC. DIAND.
p. 40 (bottom, e002213341) LAC. S. J. Bailey.
p. 41 (top, bottom) Adopt Indian Métis (AIM) Program.
p. 42 (bottom) Adopt Indian Métis (AIM) Program.
p. 42 (top) Kent Monkman. *The Scoop*, 2018.
p. 42 (middle) Provincial Archives of Saskatchewan.
p. 43 (top right) Adam North Peigan.
p. 43 (top left) *New Breed Newspaper*.
p. 46 (left, right) Adam North Peigan.
p. 47 (top left, top right, middle, bottom) Angela Ashawasegai.
p. 48 (top) Eric Stewart.
p. 48 (middle) Patrick Stewart.
p. 48 (bottom) Sharon Gladue-Paskimin.
p. 49 (top, e010691064) LAC. DIAND.
p. 49 (middle, e010969131) LAC. Health and Welfare Canada.
p. 49 (bottom) Sharon Gladue-Paskimin.
p. 50 (top, middle) Maya Cousineau Mollen.
p. 50 (bottom, PA-140582) LAC. Richard Harrington.
p. 51 (top, e010975584) LAC. NFBC.
p. 51 (bottom left) Christin Dennis.
p. 51 (bottom right, PA-117945) LAC.
p. 52 (top left, PA-114679) LAC.
p. 52 (middle, bottom right) Tauni Sheldon.
p. 53 (top left, top right) Colleen Heely.
p. 53 (bottom right, bottom left) Carla Harris.
p. 54 (top left) American Indian Movement.
p. 54 (middle, e011065953) Duncan Cameron.
p. 54 (bottom left) *Minneapolis Star Tribune*. Charles Bjorgen.
p. 55 (top left, J-547) *The Edmonton Journal*.
p. 55 (middle top) Howard Adams. *Tortured People: The Politics of Colonization*, 2002.
p. 55 (top right, R1044, RG33-115) LAC. DIAND.
p. 55 (bottom left, PA-193380) Duncan Cameron.
p. 55 (bottom right) Maria Campbell. *Halfbreed*.
p. 56 (left, right) Kina Gbezhgomi. Child and Family Services.
p. 57 (top) Dilico Anishinabek Family Care.
p. 57 (bottom left) Native Child and Family Services of Toronto.
p. 57 (middle left) Kingsclear Child and Family Services.
p. 57 (middle right) Athabasca Tribal Council.
p. 57 (bottom right) Mi'kmaq Confederacy of PEI.
p. 58 (left) The University of Manitoba Archives and Special Collections.
p. 58 (left) *No Quiet Place* (Kimelman Report).

p. 59 (top, bottom) LAC. Ministère de la Santé nationale et du Bien-être.
p. 60 (left) Isaac Murdoch. *Child's Dream*.
p. 60 (right) National Centre for Truth and Reconciliation Archives.
p. 61 (top) Flickr. Justin Trudeau.
p. 61 (middle) National Centre for Truth and Reconciliation Archives.
p. 61 (bottom) Librarianship.ca.
p. 63 (bottom) Flickr. Justin Trudeau.
p. 64 (left) *Winnipeg Free Press*.
p. 64 (right) Manitoba Archives.
p. 65 (right) Manitoba Archives.
p. 65 (bottom) City News.
p. 66 Ontario Association of Children's Aid Societies.
p. 67 (top) Government of Alberta.
p. 67 (bottom) Government of Saskatchewan.
p. 68-69 Government of Saskatchewan.
p. 70 (top left) *The Manitoulin Expositor*, 2017.
p. 70 (top right, bottom) LOHF.
p. 71 (top) Ontario Supreme Court of Justice. Brown v. Canada class action lawsuit.
p. 71 (bottom) The Canadian Press.
p. 72 (top) Jillian Kestler-D'Amours, 2017.
p. 72 (middle) LOHF.
p. 72-73 (bottom) *Alberta Native News*.
p. 73 (top) Colin Perkel. The Canadian Press.
p. 73 (middle) Colin Perkel. The Canadian Press.
p. 74 (top) Sixties Scoop Settlement Class Action.
p. 74 (bottom) Sixties Scoop Settlement Info.
p. 75 (top) Phil Heidenreich, 2018.
p. 75 (middle) CBC News, June 2020.
p. 75 (bottom) Katie Hyslop, 2021.
p. 76-78 LOHF.
p. 79 (top) Richard Froese, 2019.
p. 79 (bottom) Conrad Prince.
p. 80 LOHF.
p. 81 (top) Brent Wesley.
p. 81 (bottom) Mang Kiki.
p. 82 LOHF.
p. 83 Mang Kiki.
p. 85 (top) The First Nations Child and Family Caring Society of Canada.
p. 85 (bottom) Flickr.
p. 86 (top, 458240811; bottom, 1270997661) iStock.
p. 87 (top) LOHF.
p. 87 (bottom) Stan Williams.
p. 88 (top, bottom) The First Nations Child and Family Caring Society of Canada.
p. 89 (top) The Canadian Press.
p. 89 (bottom) Cindy Blackstock.
p. 90 (top) TB News Watch.
p. 90 (bottom) Anna McMillan, February 2021.
p. 92 Shutterstock.
p. 93 (top) Canadian Human Rights Tribunal website.
p. 93 (bottom) Indigenous Services Canada.
p. 94 (left) Sarah Cardinal Wright.
p. 94 (right) Qikiqtani Inuit Association.
P. 95 (top left) Angela Ashawasegai.
p. 95 (top right) National Film Board. *Birth of a Family*, 2017.
p. 95 (bottom left, bottom right) LOHF.
p. 96 (top) Flickr. Vancouver School Board.
p. 96 (bottom) Flickr. Mike Clothier.
p. 97 (top) Flickr.
p. 97 (middle, 1028895538) iStock.
p. 97 (bottom) LOHF.
p. 98 (top, bottom) LAC. George Mully.
p. 99 (top, 157618857) iStock.
p. 99 (bottom) LOHF.
p. 100 (1337046832) iStock.
p. 101 (top) Isaac Murdoch. Children Home Tipi.
p. 101 (bottom) Government of Canada, 2010.
p. 102 (top, bottom) Flickr. Justin Trudeau.
p. 103 (top) Flickr. Justin Trudeau.
p. 103 (bottom left) Alicia McDonald.
p. 103 (bottom right) Penguin First Nation.

Acknowledgements

We would like to personally acknowledge and thank the following people for their contributions to this book. Without their willingness to share their experience, strength, hope and time, this book would not have been possible. We honour each and every one of you.

Survivors
Adam North Peigan
Eric Stewart
Patrick Stewart
Sharon Gladue-Paskimin
Maya Cousineau Mollen
Christin Dennis
Brent Mitchell
Tauni Sheldon
Carla Harris
Angela Ashawasegai
Nina Segalowitz

We would like to thank Legacy of Hope Foundation staff and former staff who helped with the preparation of the text and visuals in this book, Danielle James, Michelle Fraser and Jane Hubbard.

Legacy of Hope Foundation volunteers who provided assistance with this project were Nathan Shaw, Simon Cavanaugh, Saja Terier, Caitlin Hung, Victoria King, Arya Joshi, Olivia Grado, Sarah Barube, Jessica-Lynn Anderson and Sanaz Ghojeh Biglou. We thank artists Isaac Murdoch, Kent Monkman and Maya Cousineau Mollen for providing permissions for reproduction of their work in this volume. We would also like to thank publishing staff Pam Hickman and Heather Epp for their work on this book.

— TE and AB

My thanks go first and foremost to my wife, Rebekah. Her patience and support made working on this book possible. I love you very much. I also owe a huge thanks to the whole Legacy of Hope Foundation team who worked to bring this project together — this truly was a collaborative effort.

— AB

I am so happy and grateful for the support from the Legacy of Hope Foundation staff, board and all volunteers, and the Lorimer team for bringing this book to fruition to tell this important chapter in history so we may learn from it. To my children Ashley, Dakota, Derek and grandchildren Alivia, Avery, Dalila Sage, Aspen and Miah, may you always be inspired by the strength of your ancestors just as you have inspired me to be courageous in advancing human rights and freedoms, fostering Reconciliation and creating a brighter future for everyone on Turtle Island. Thank you, thank you, thank you. Gesalul.

—TE

Index

Index